Binghamton 2015: Through My Lens

Patti Schwartz

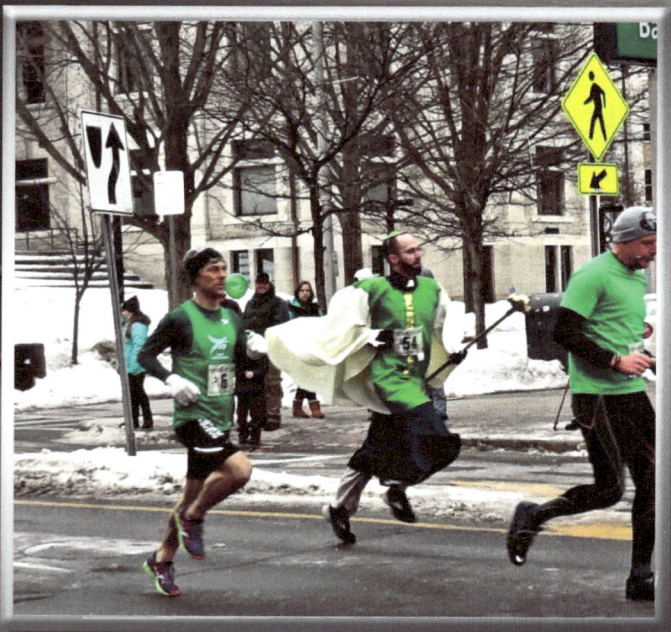
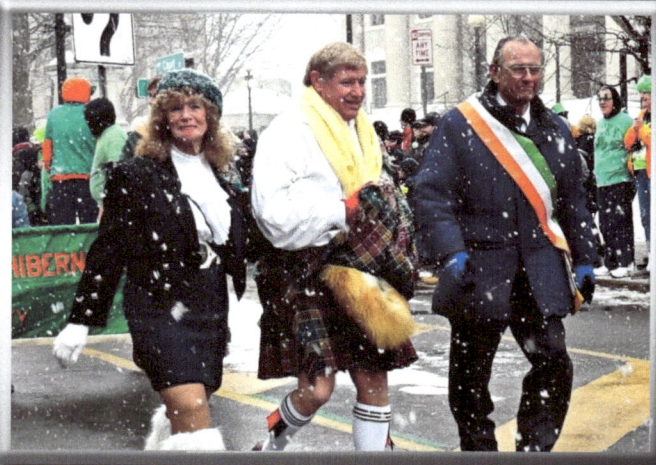
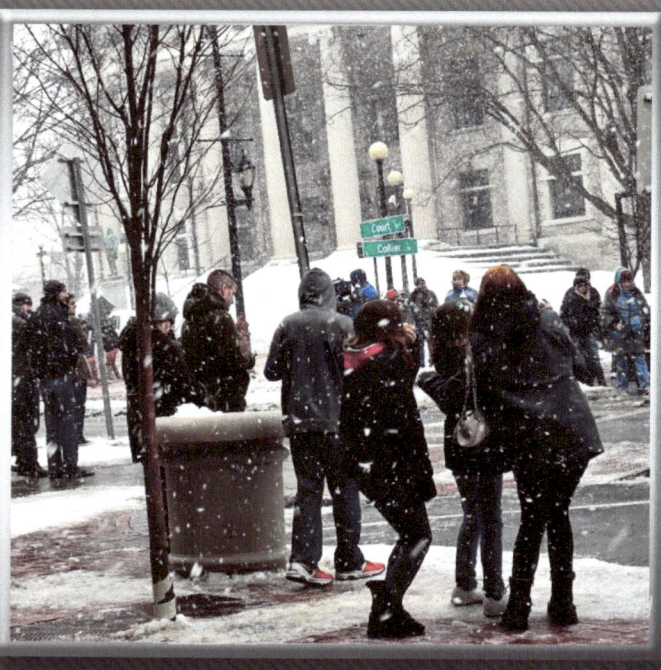
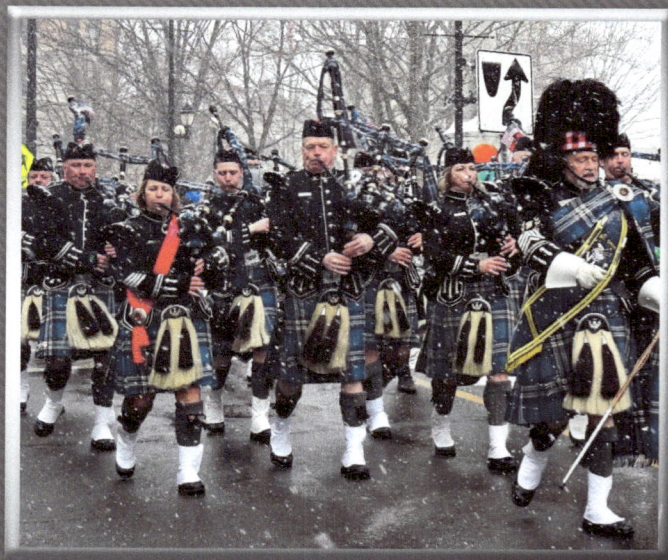

St. Patrick's Day Parade

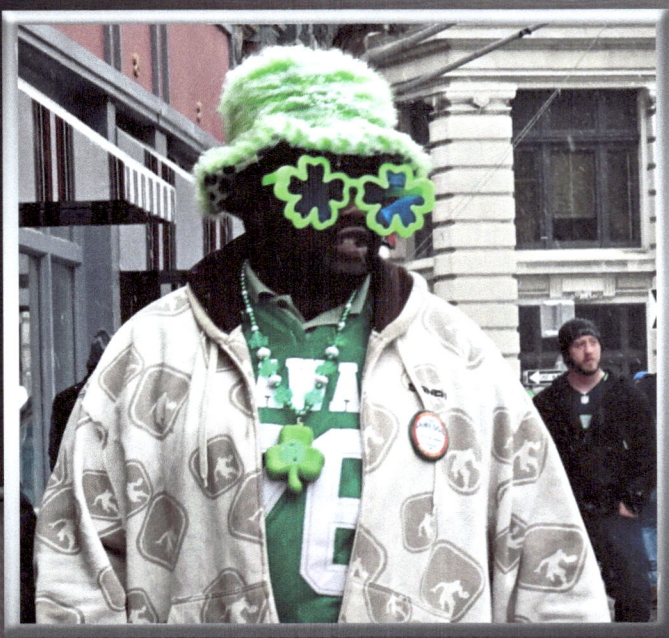
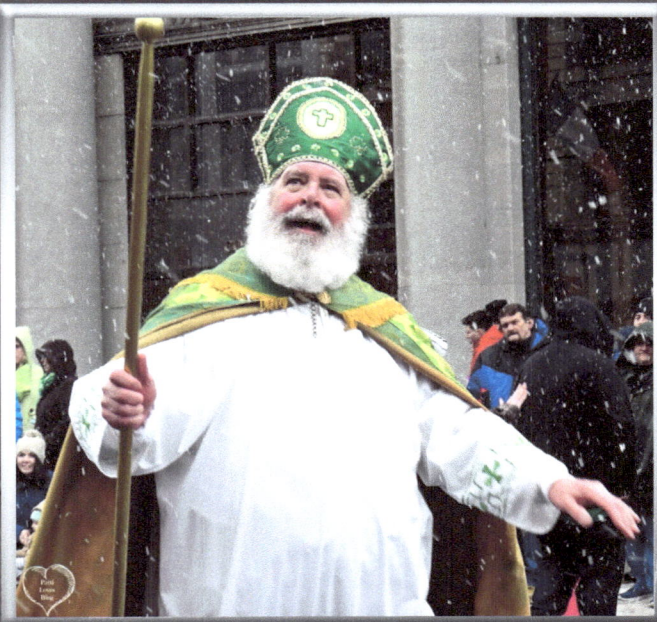
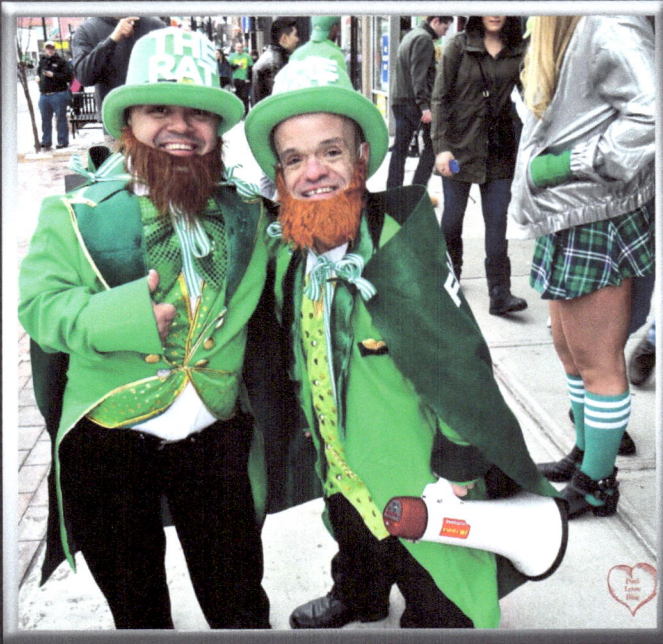
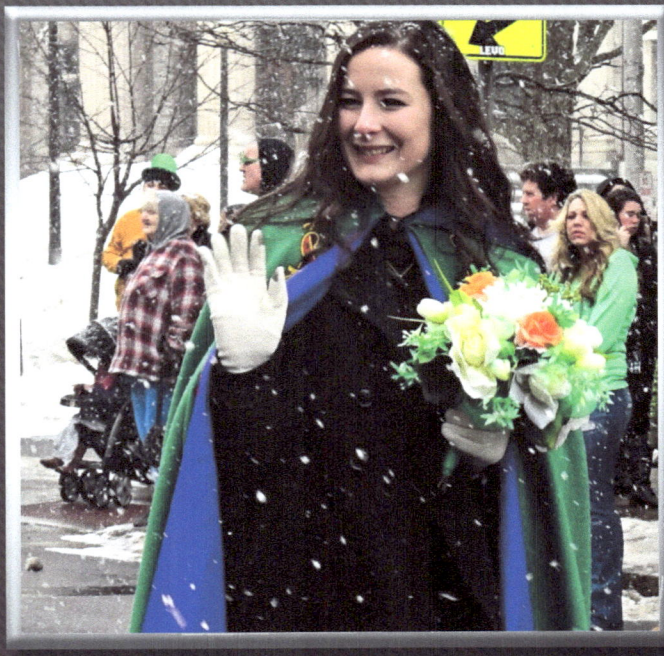

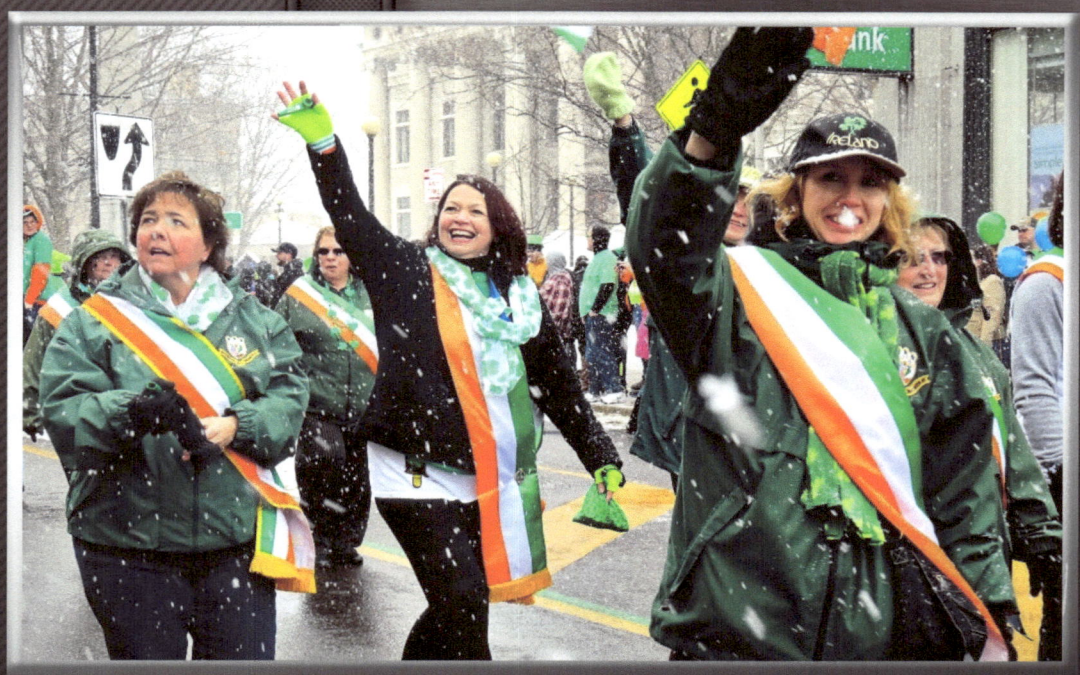
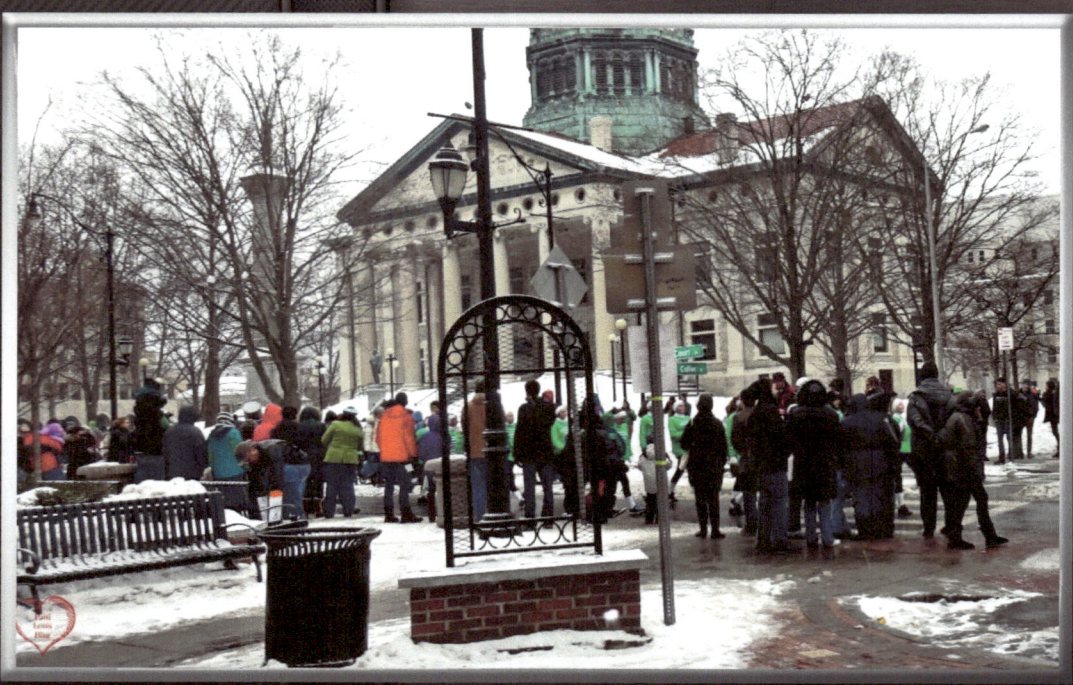

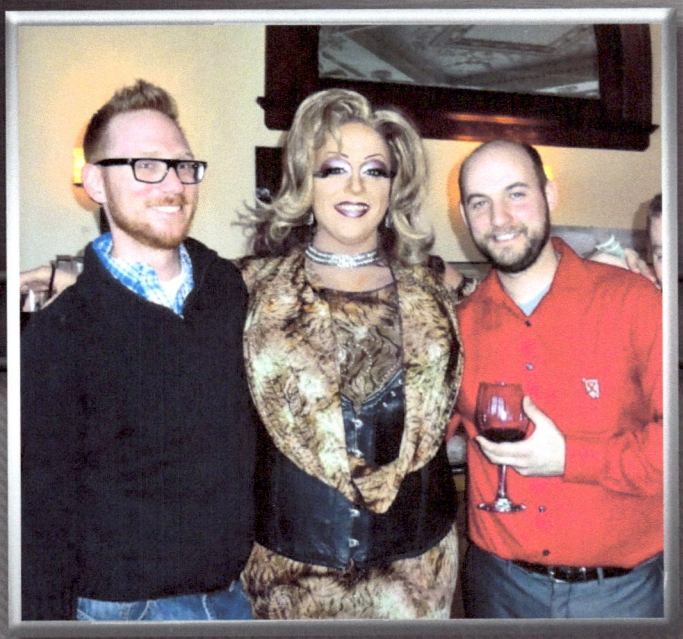
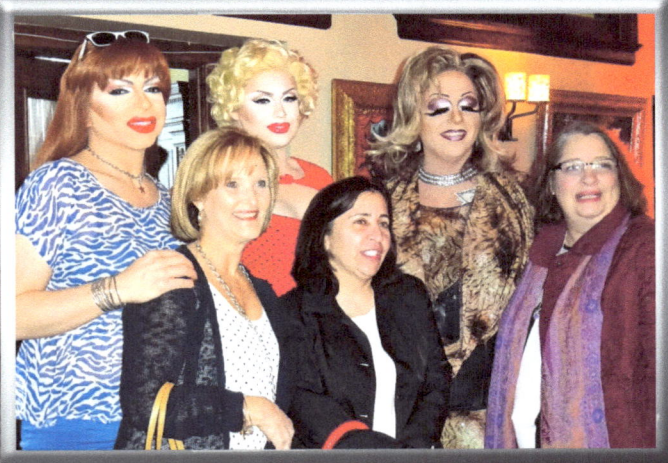
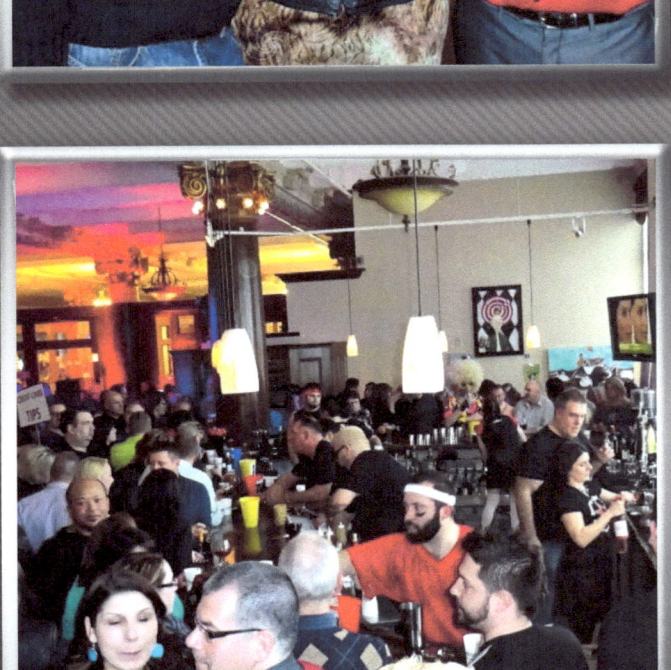
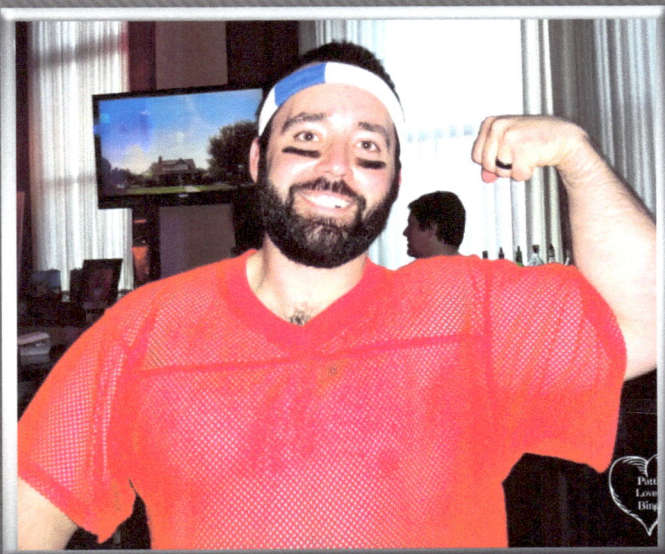

STAP Celebrity Bartending Bash

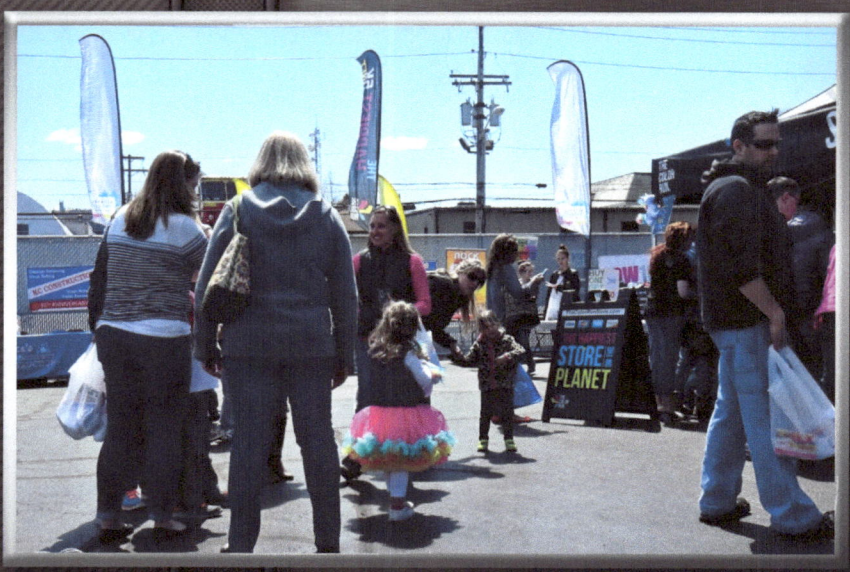
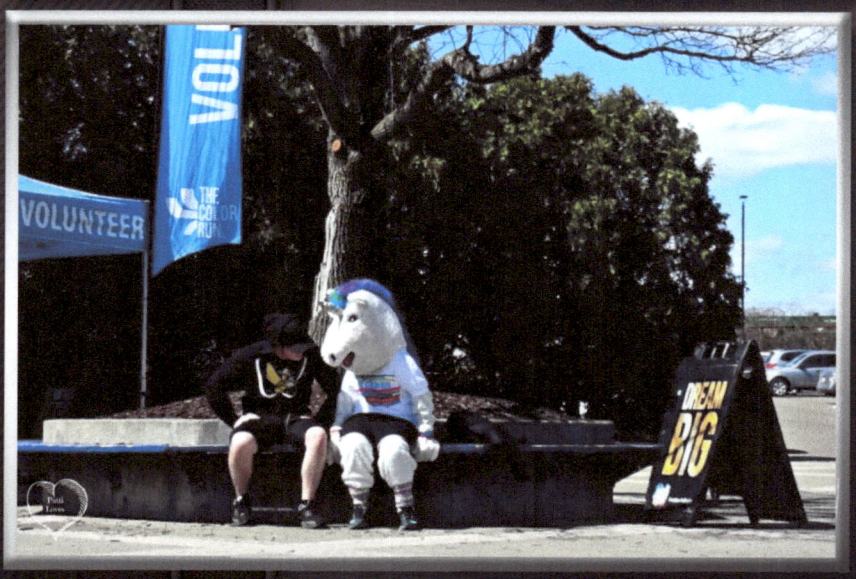

Color Run 2015
Check In Party

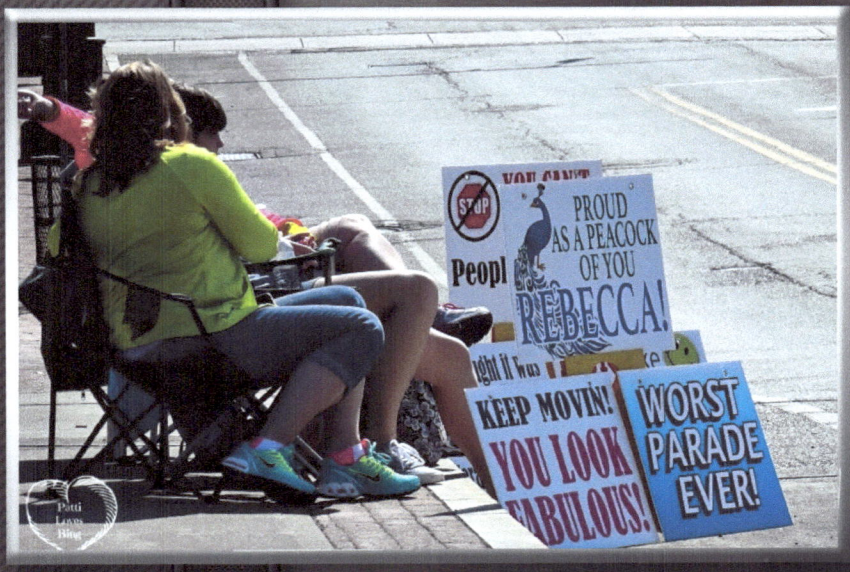
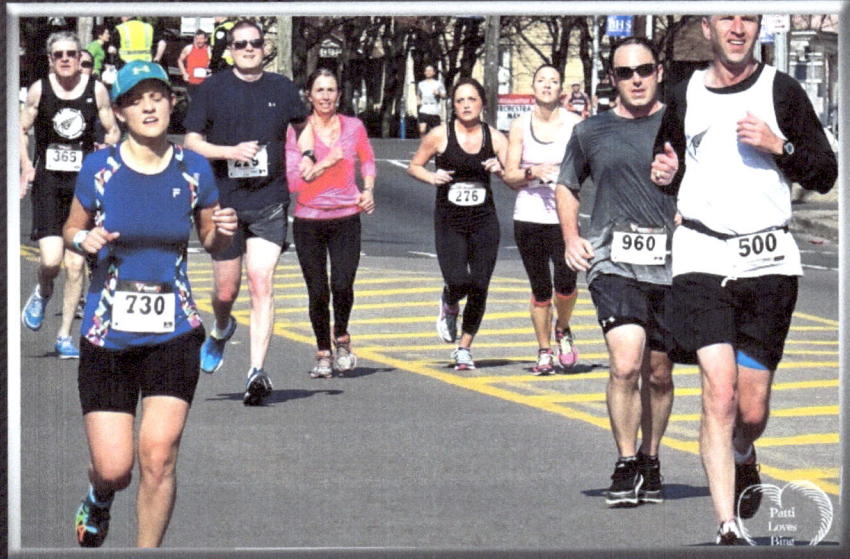

2015 Binghamton Bridge Run

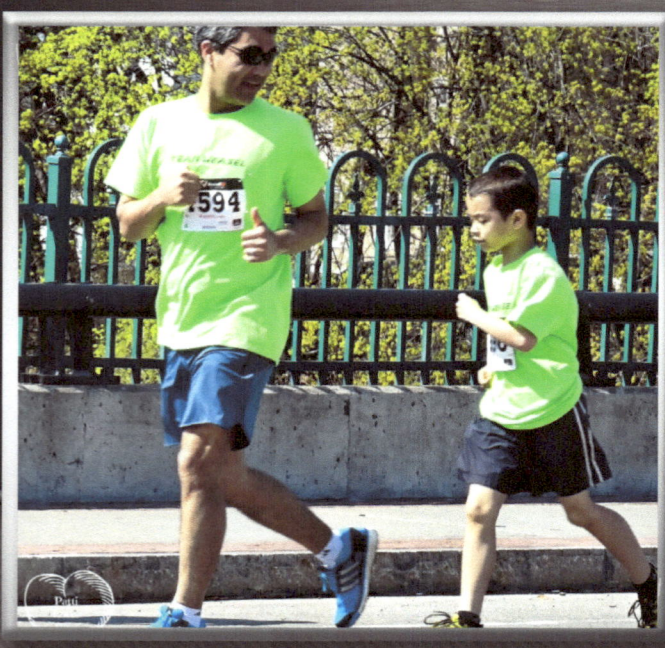
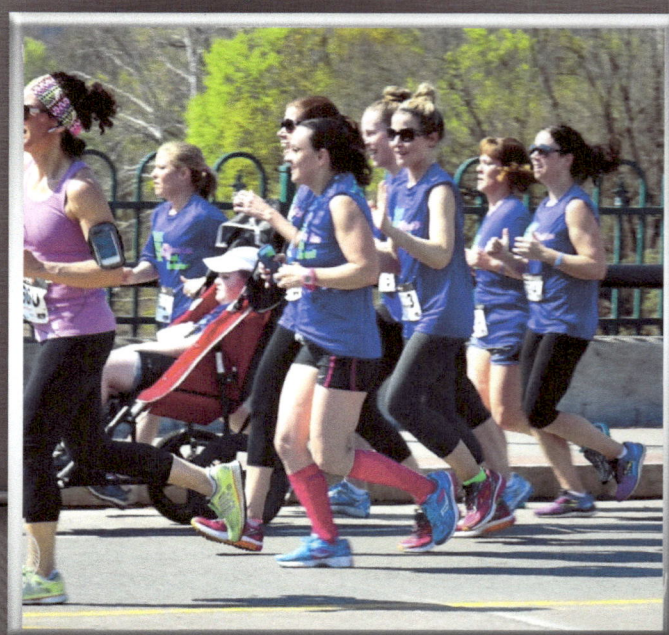
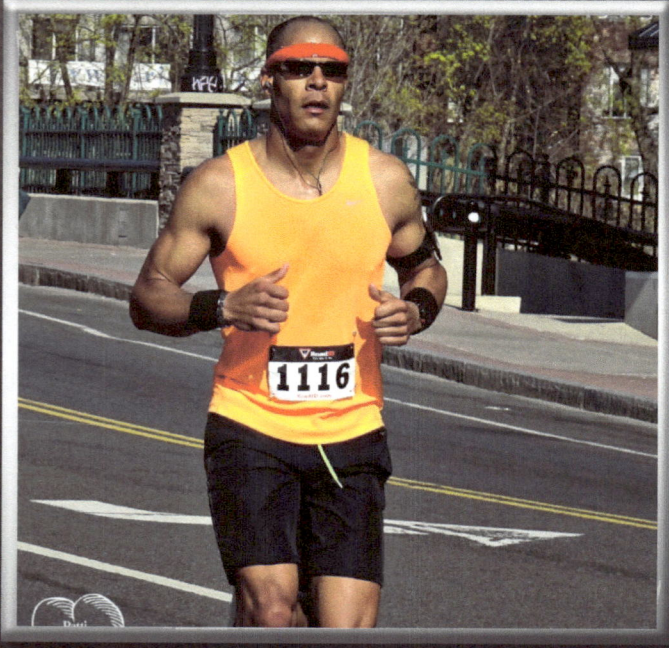
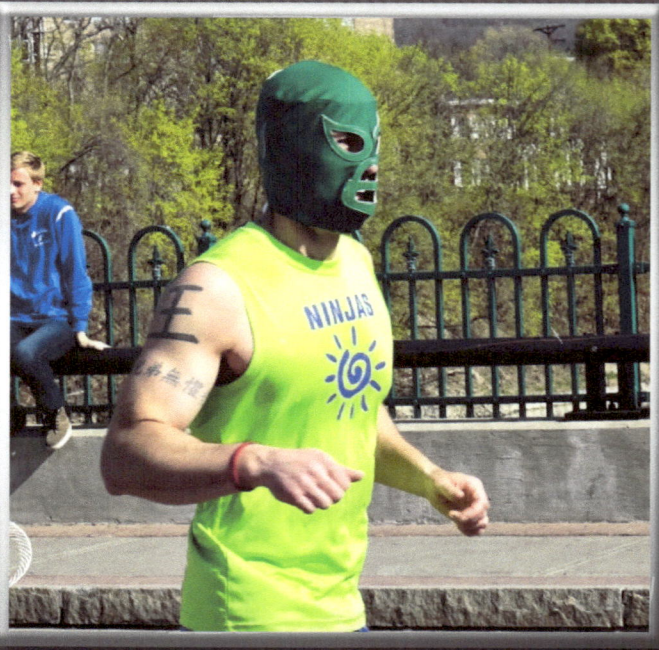

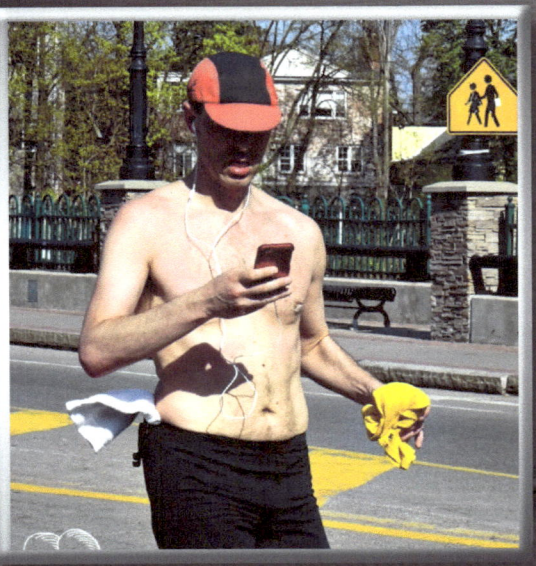
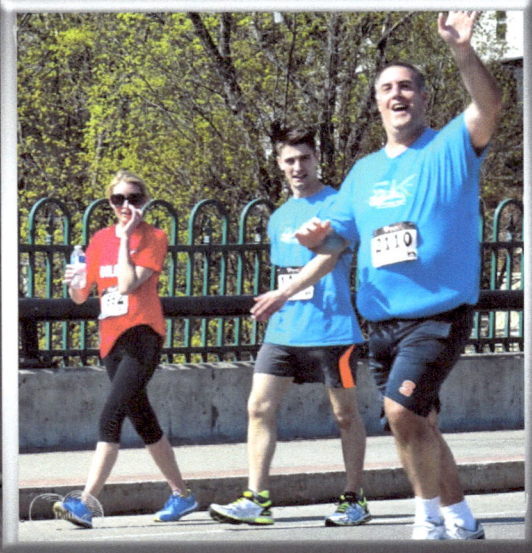
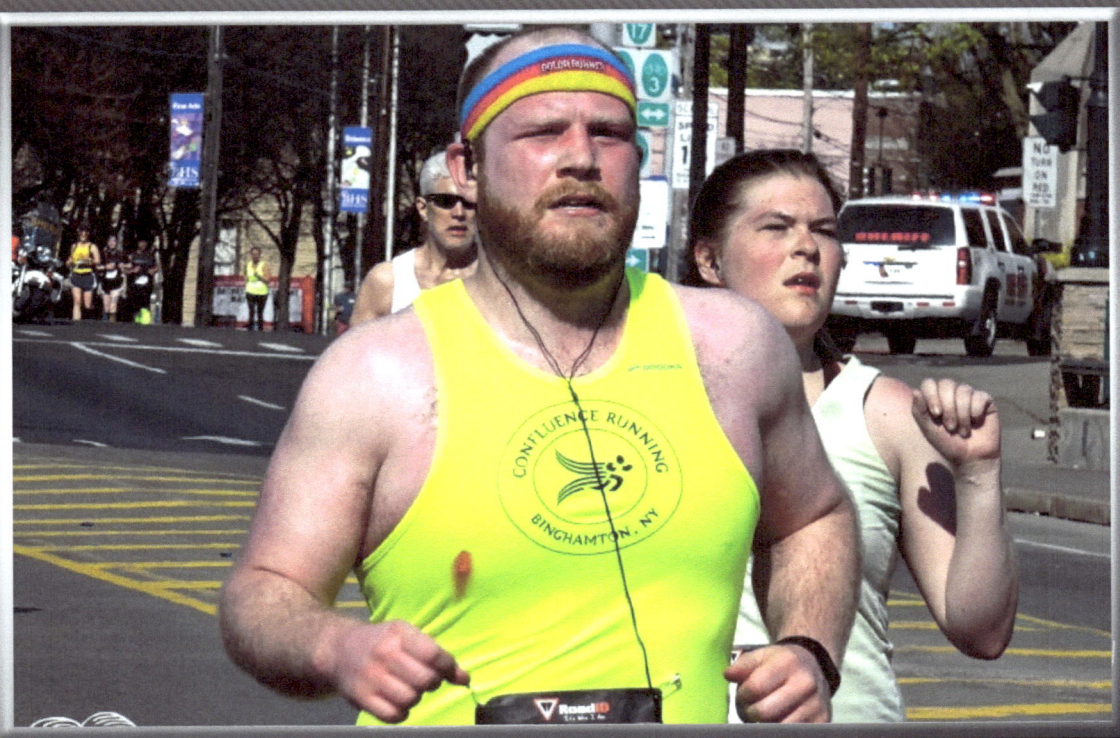

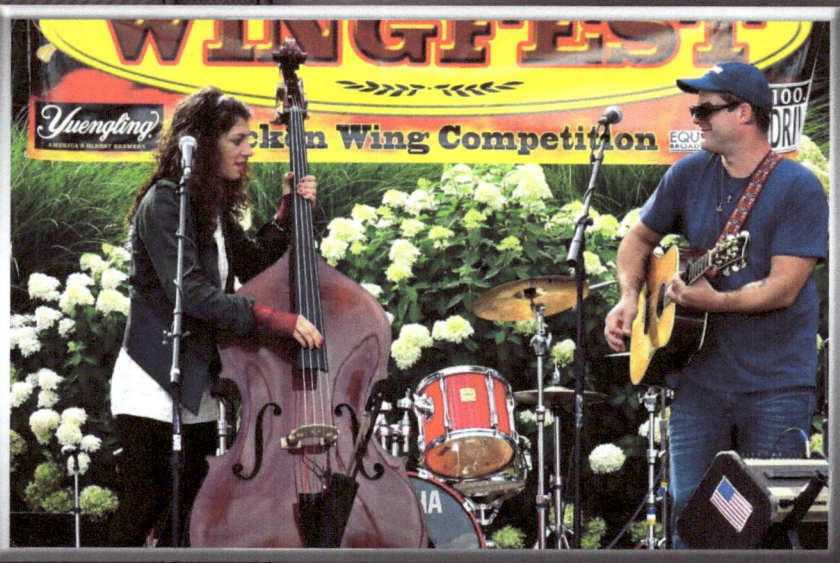

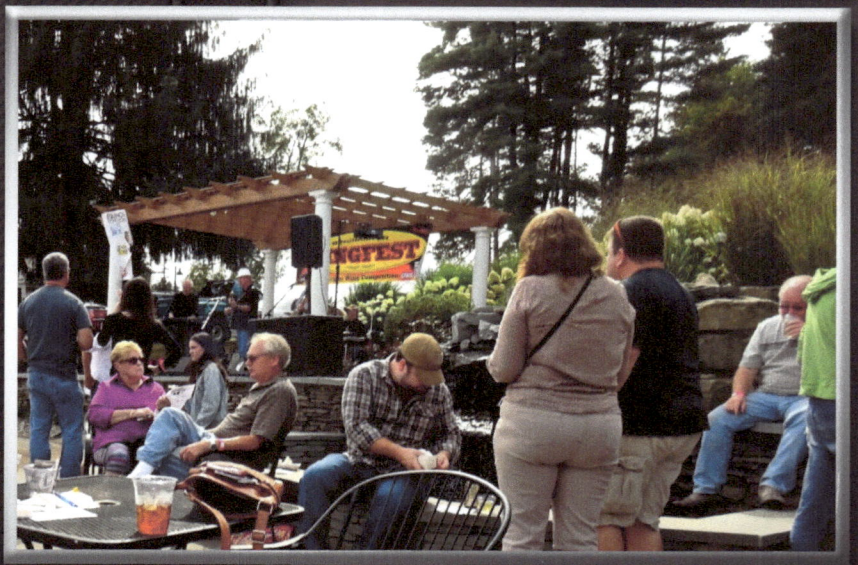

Binghamton Wingfest

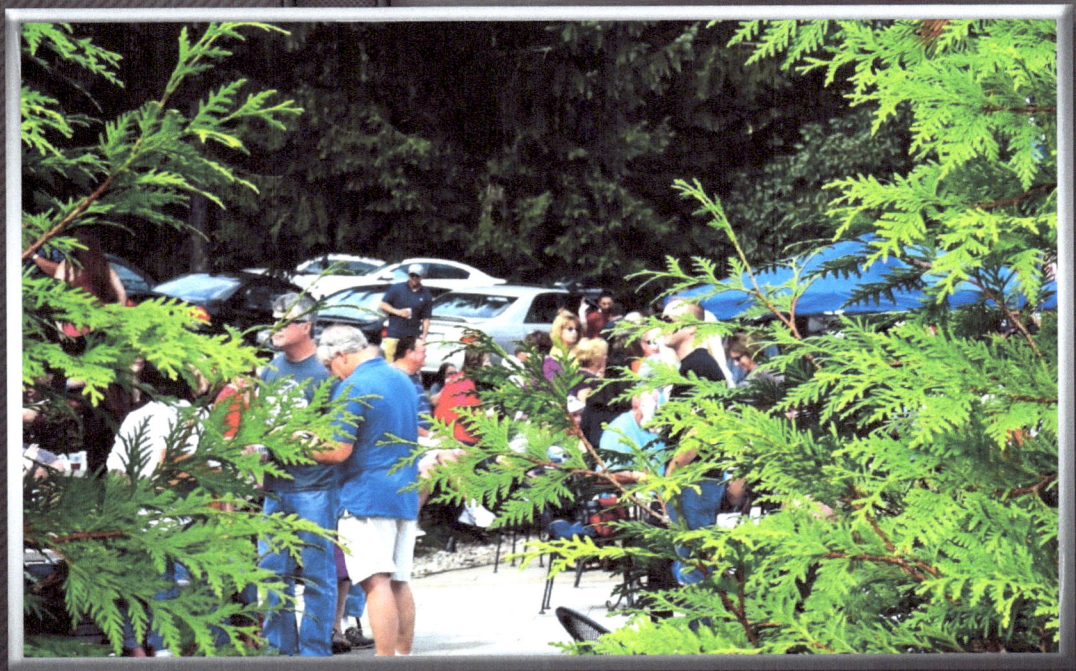
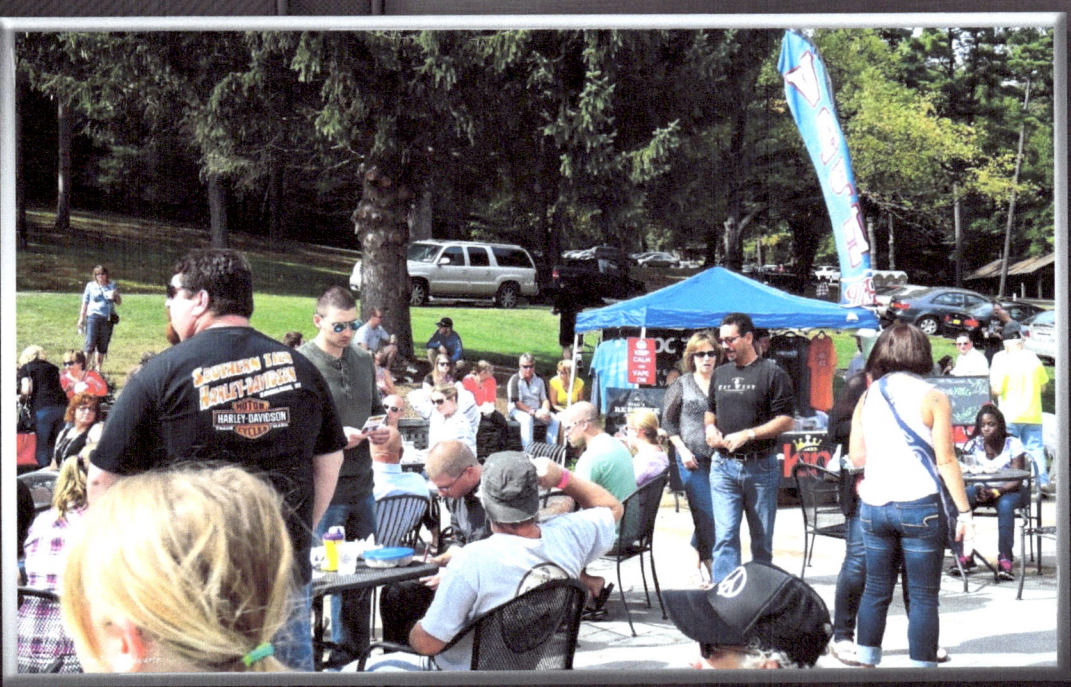

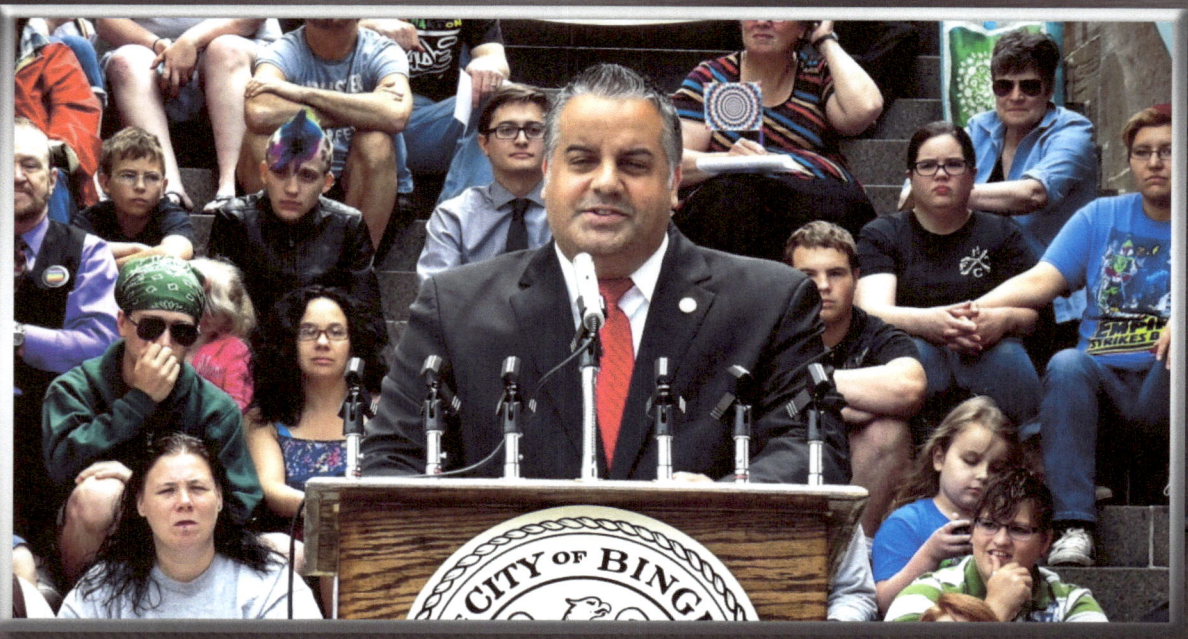
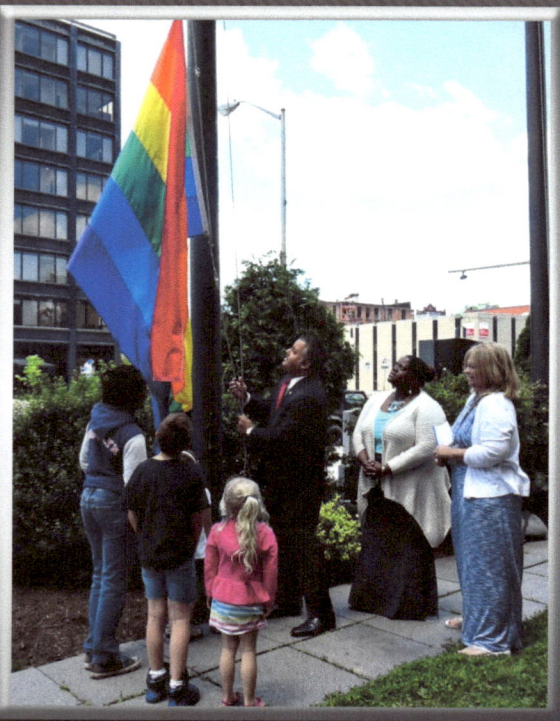
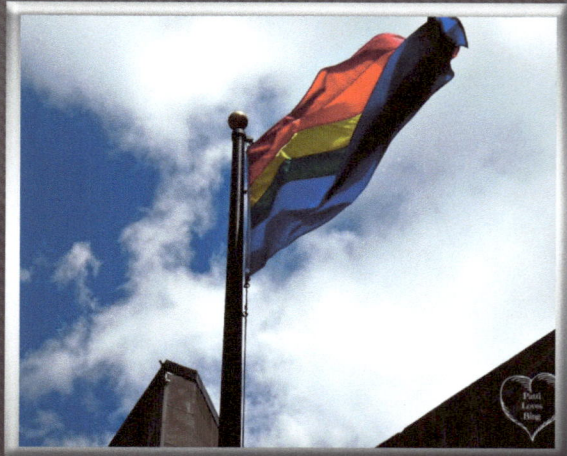

Pride Flag Raising Ceremony

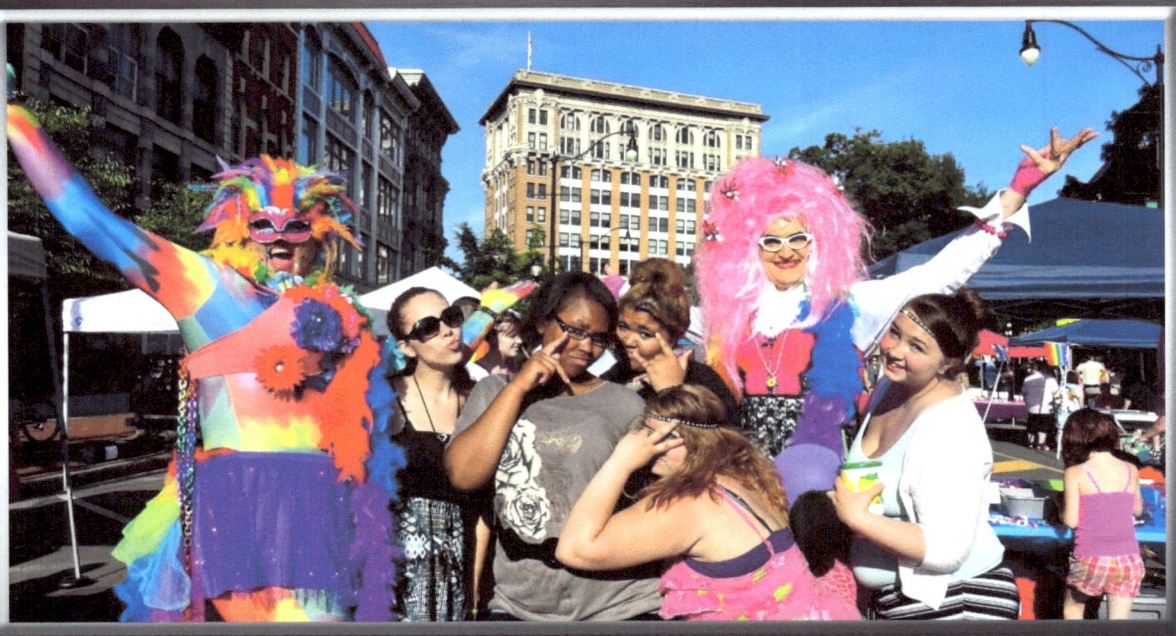
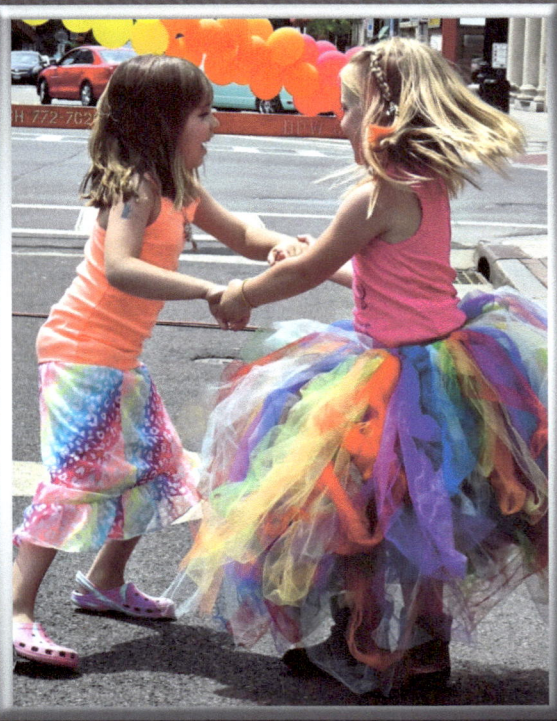
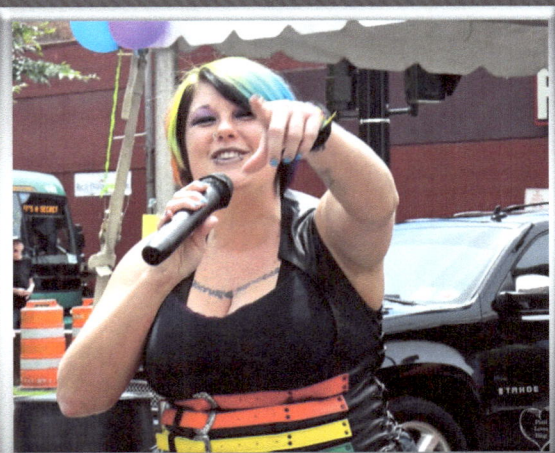

Pride Palooza 2015

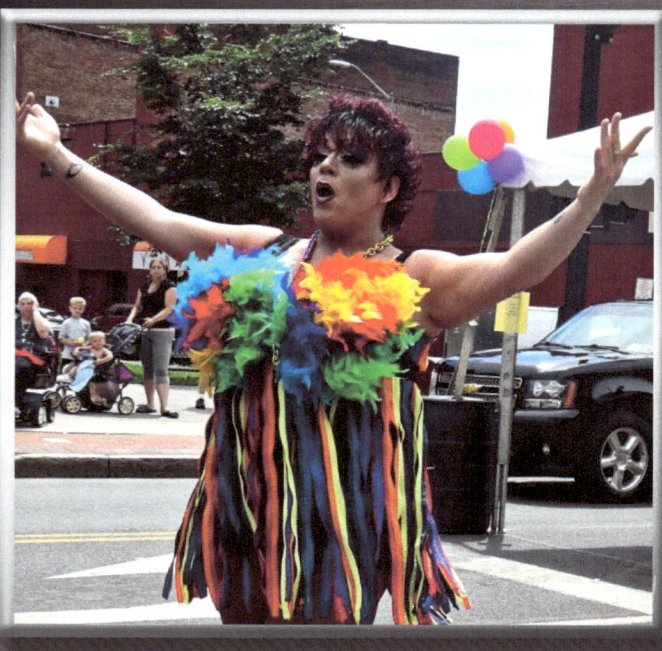
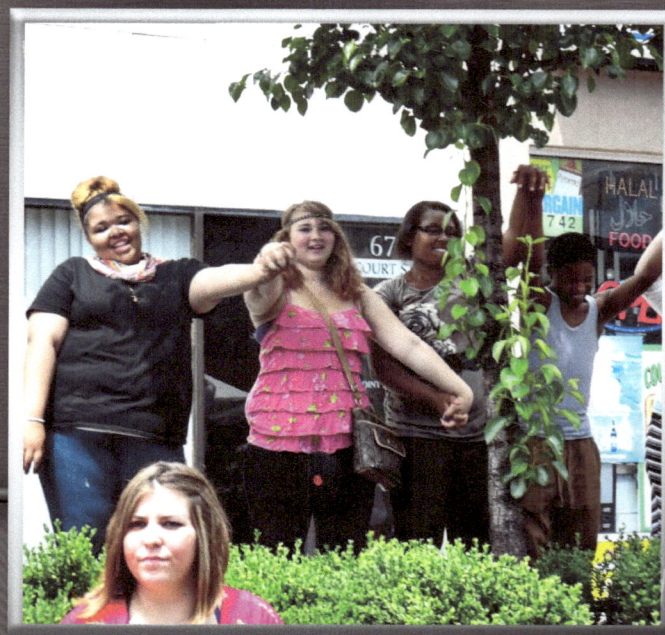
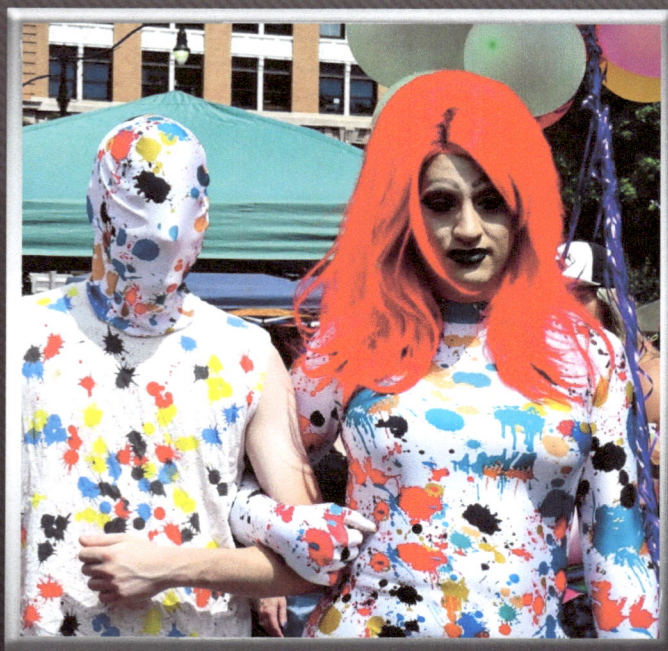
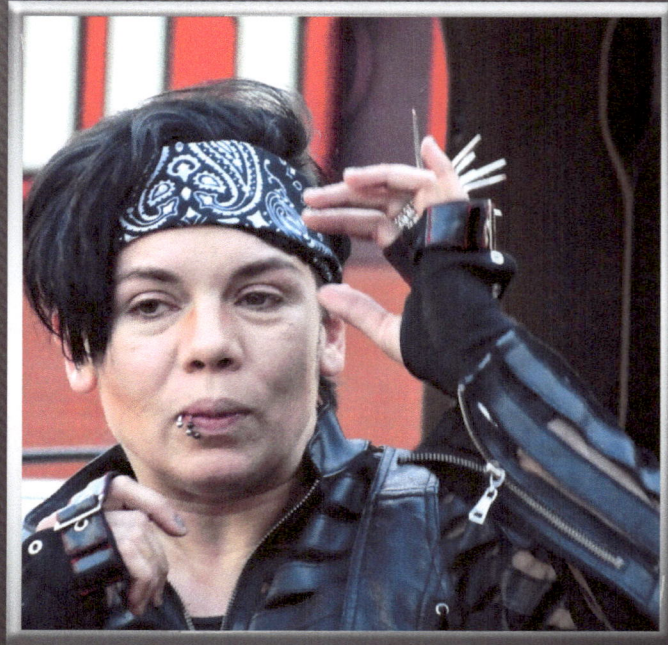

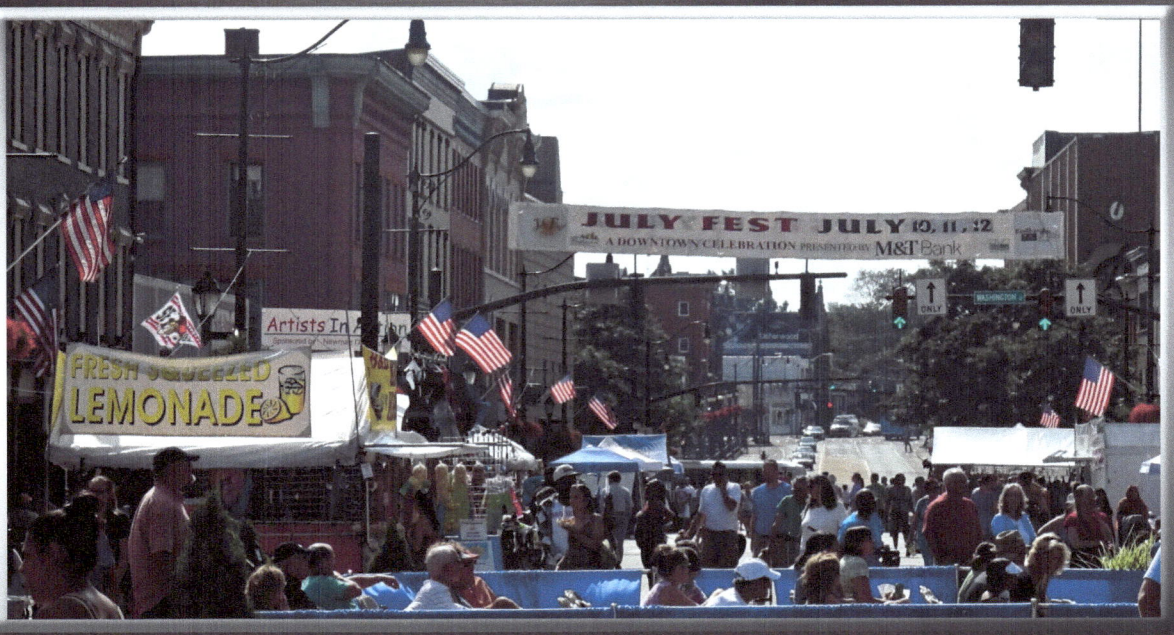
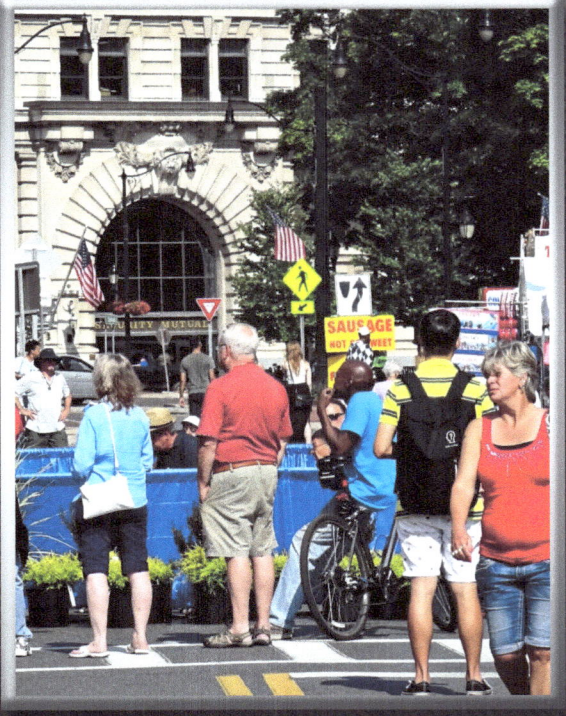
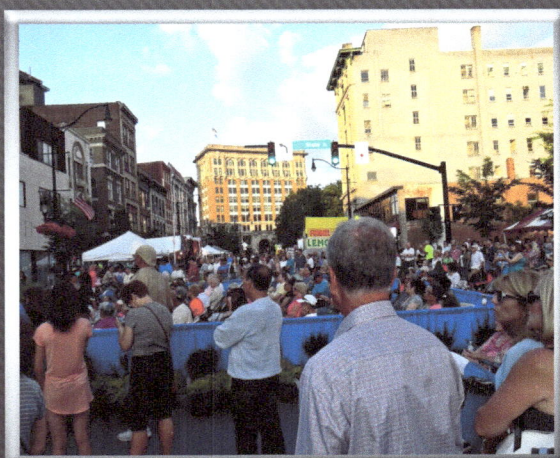

July Fest 2015

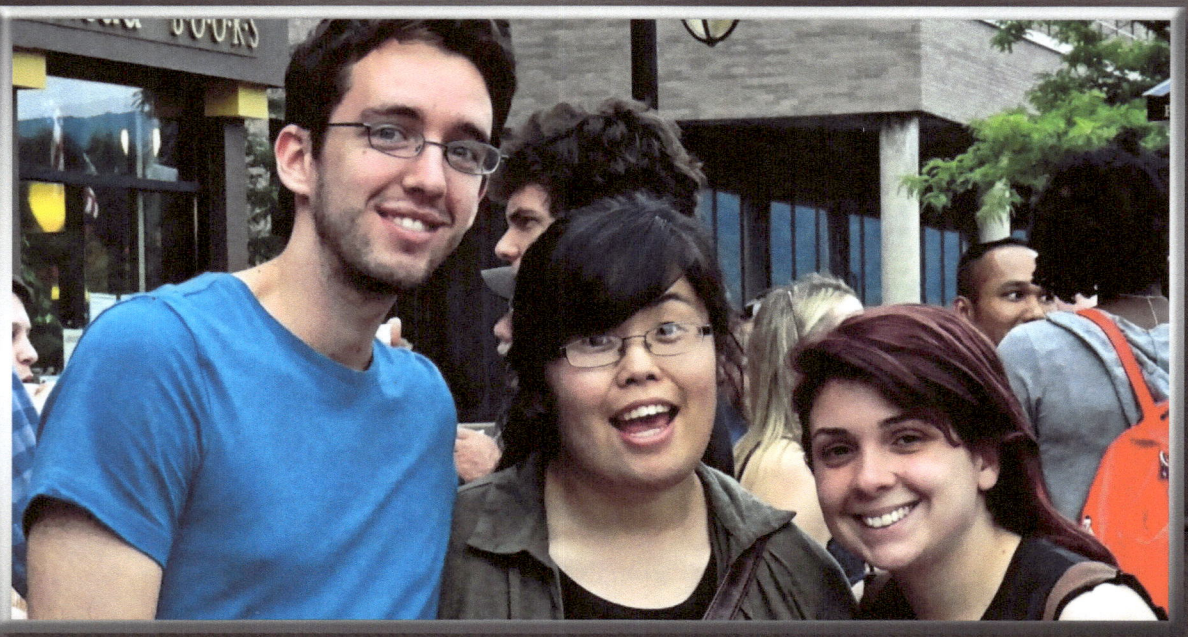
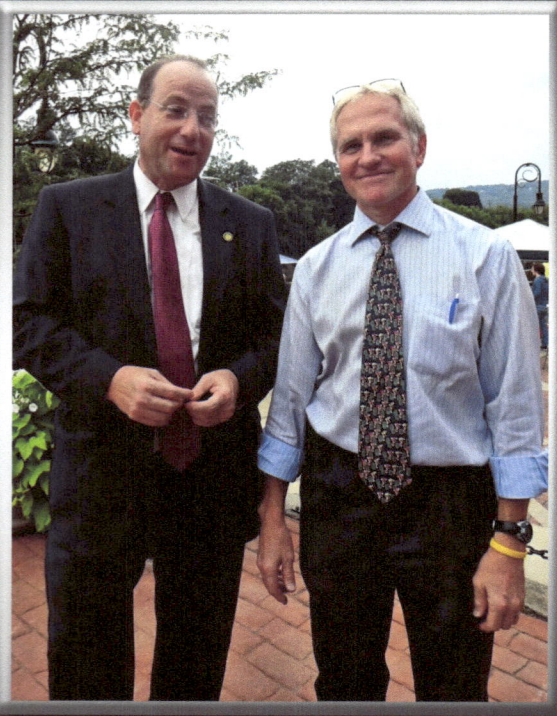
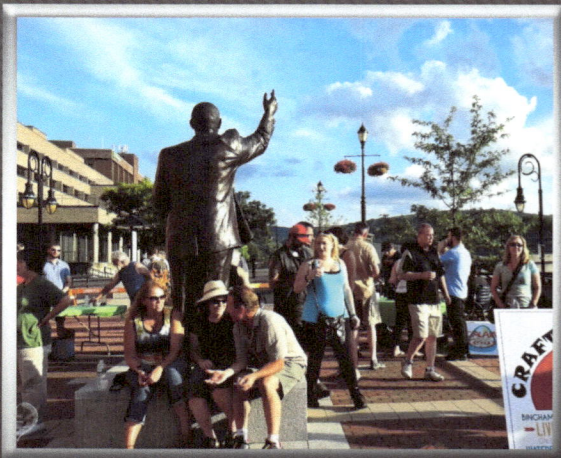

Live on the Waterfront

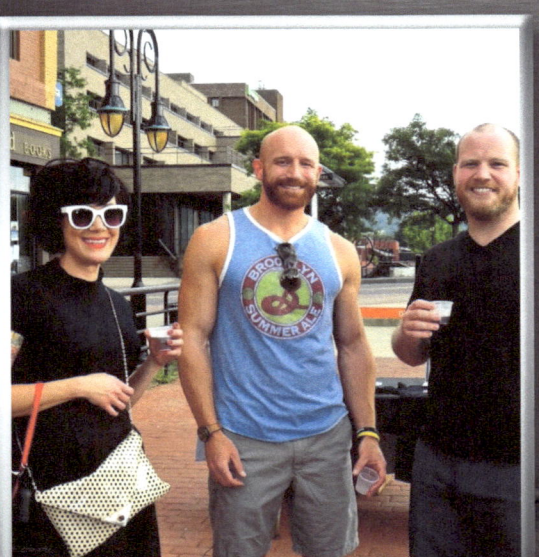
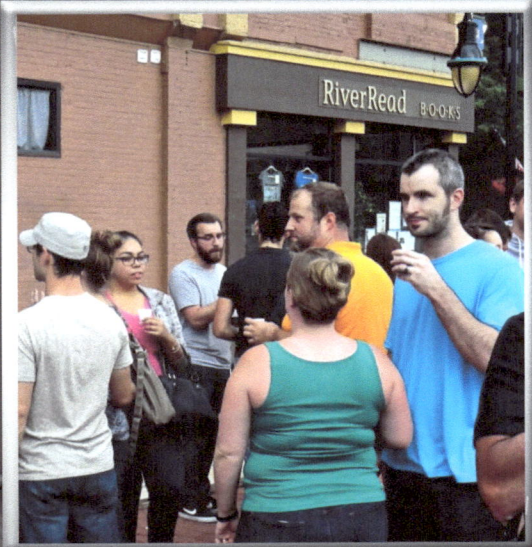
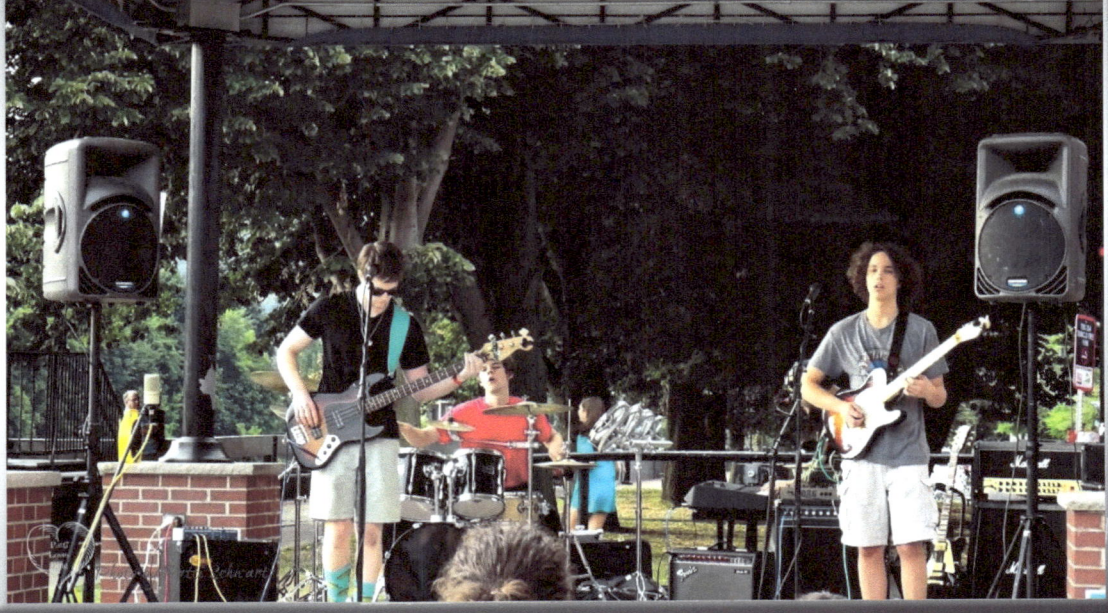

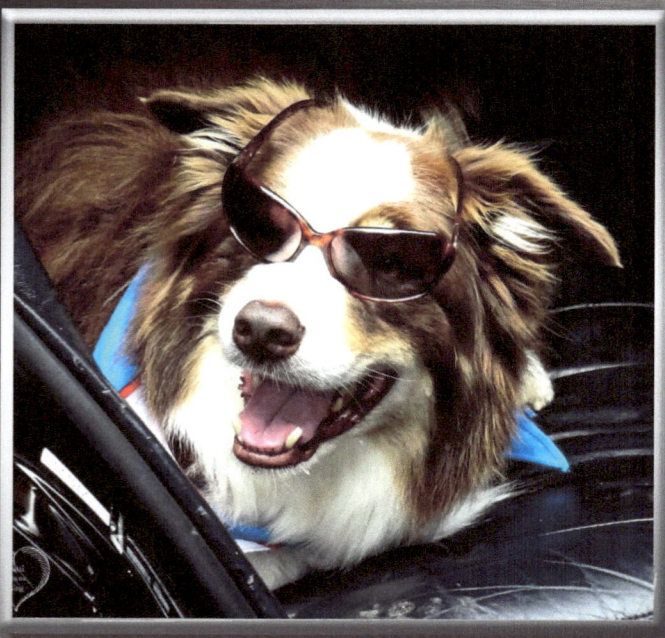
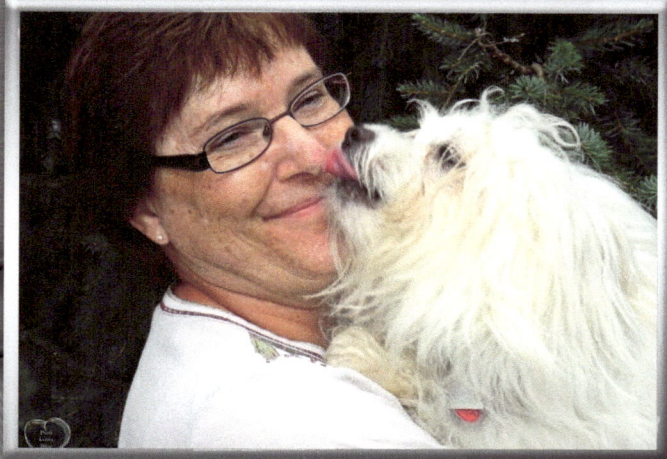
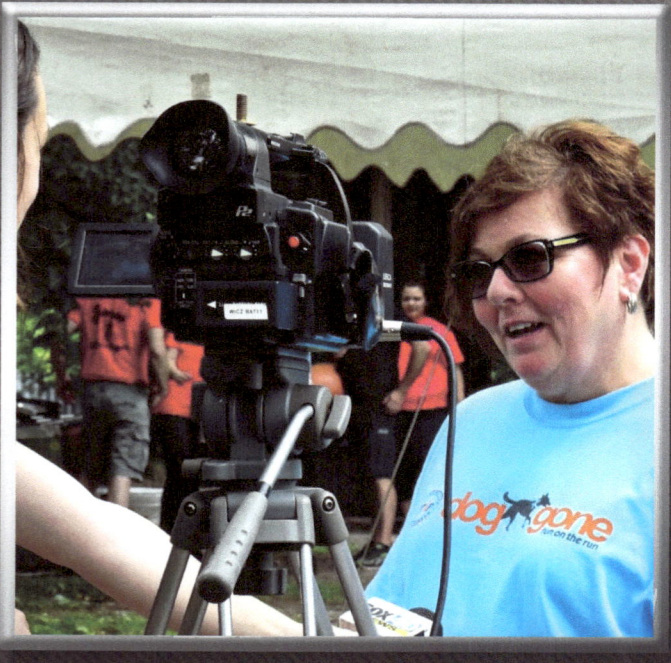
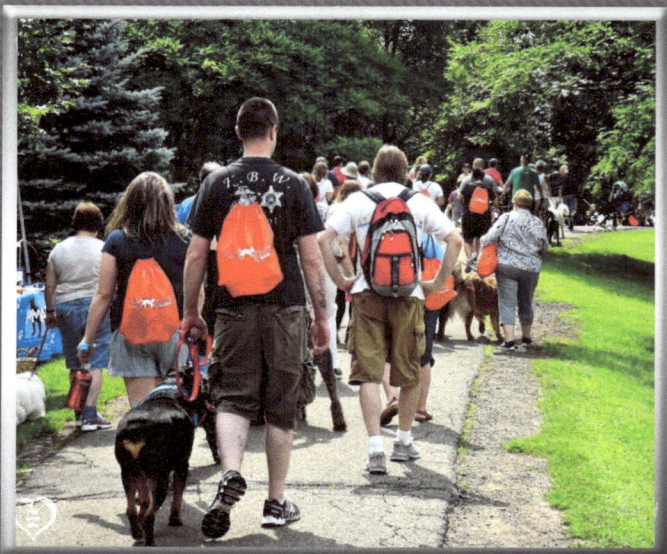

STAP Doggone Fun on the Run

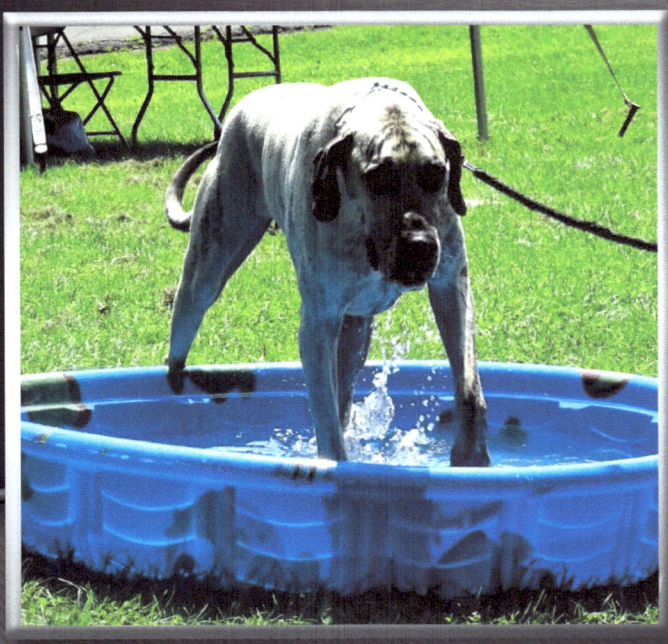
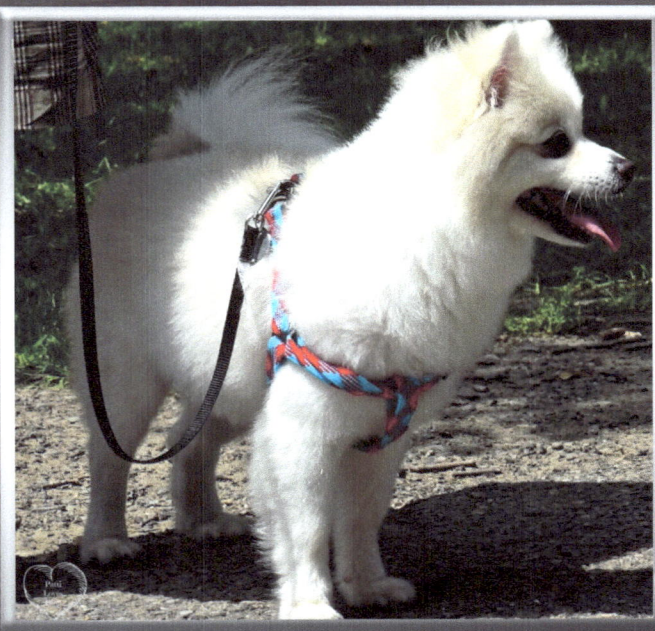
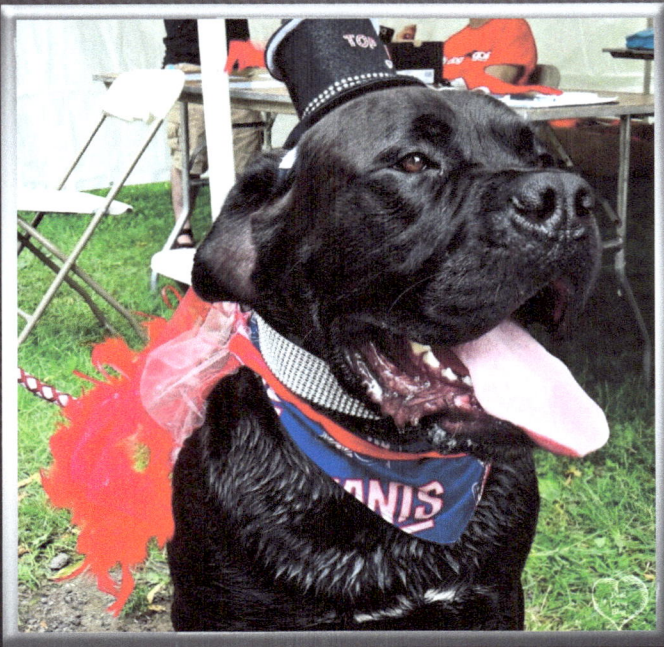
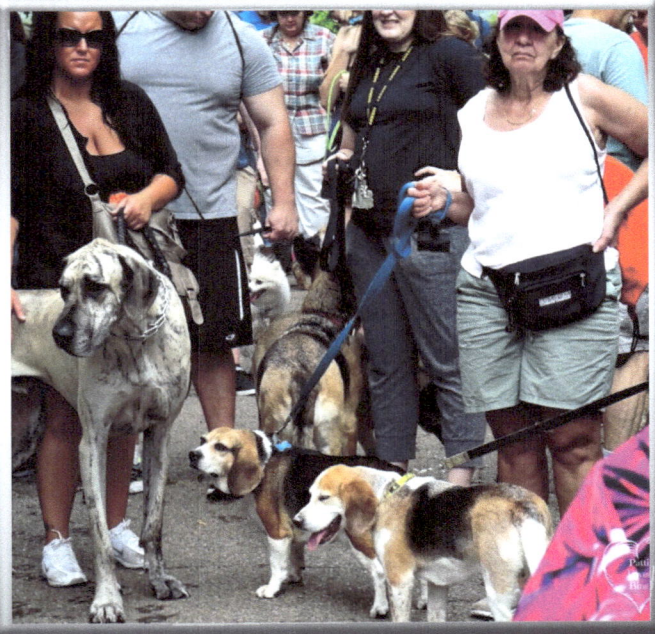

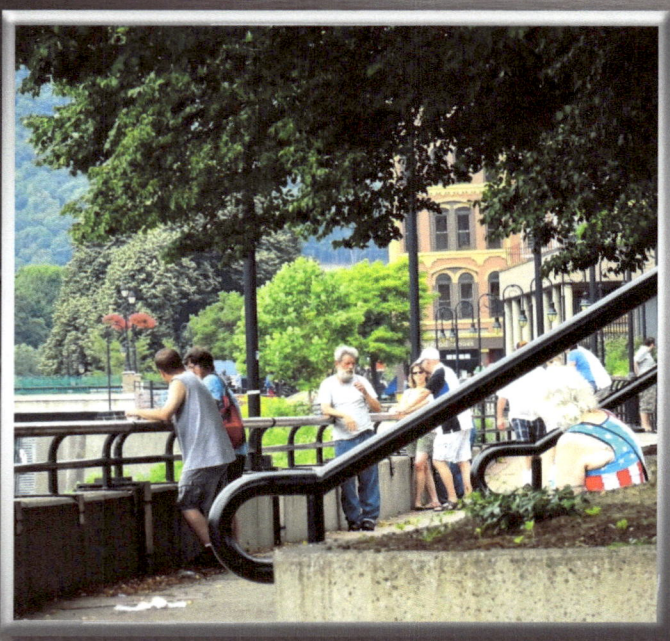
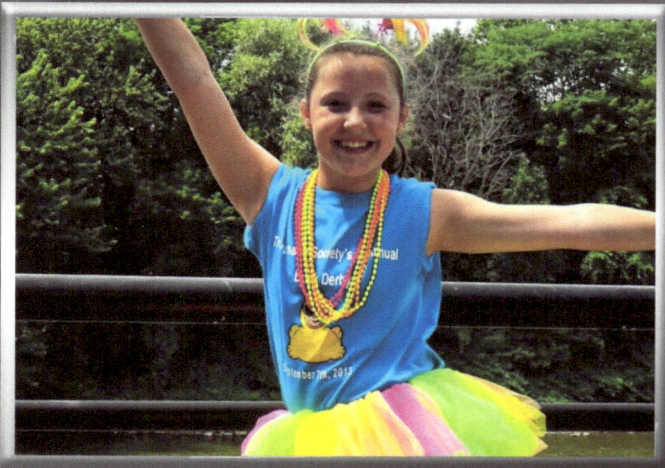
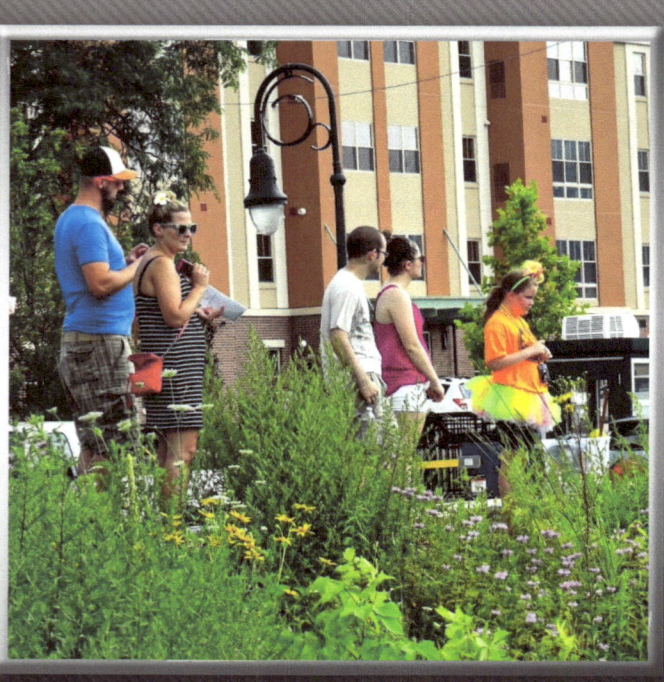
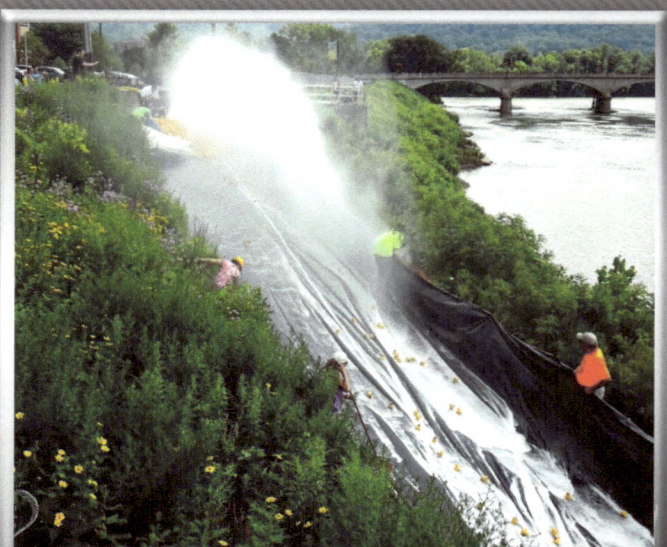

BC Humane Society Annual Duck Derby

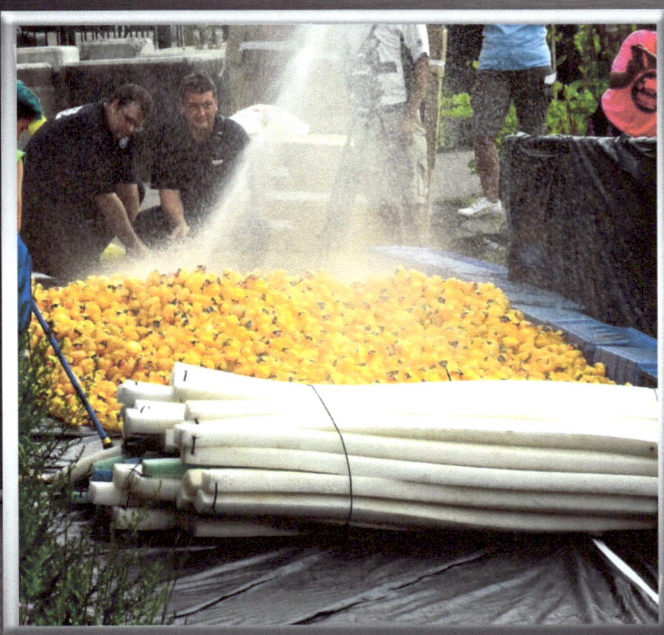
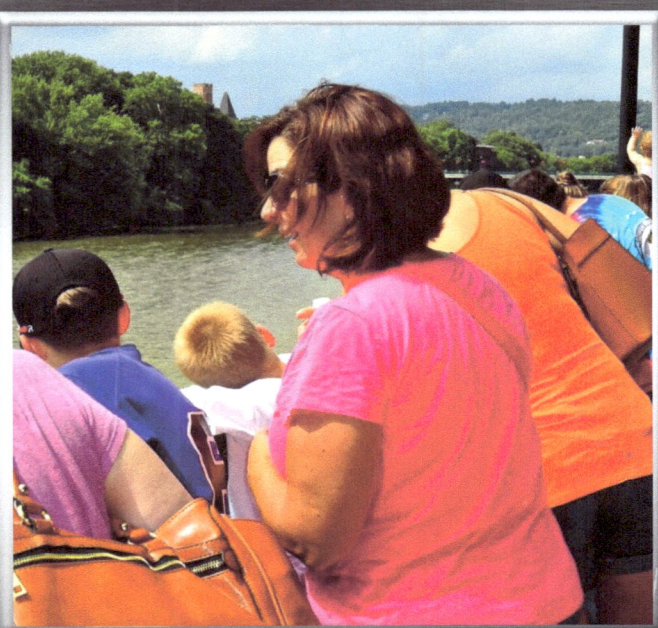
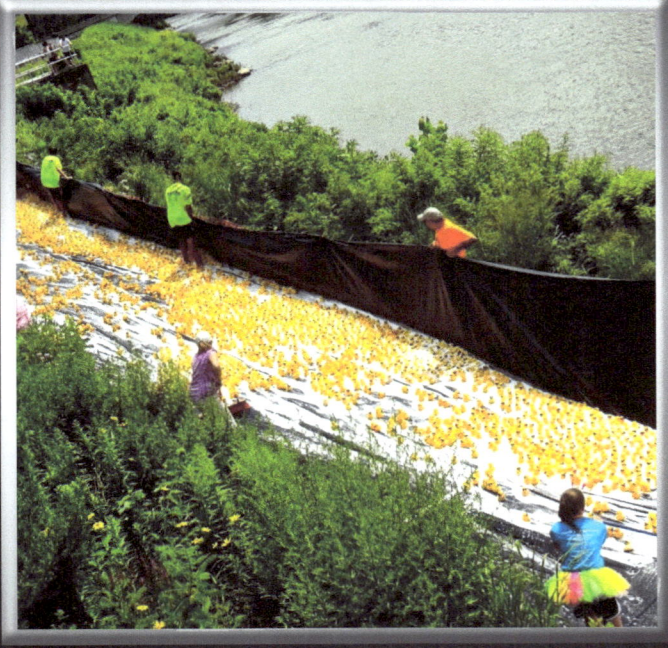
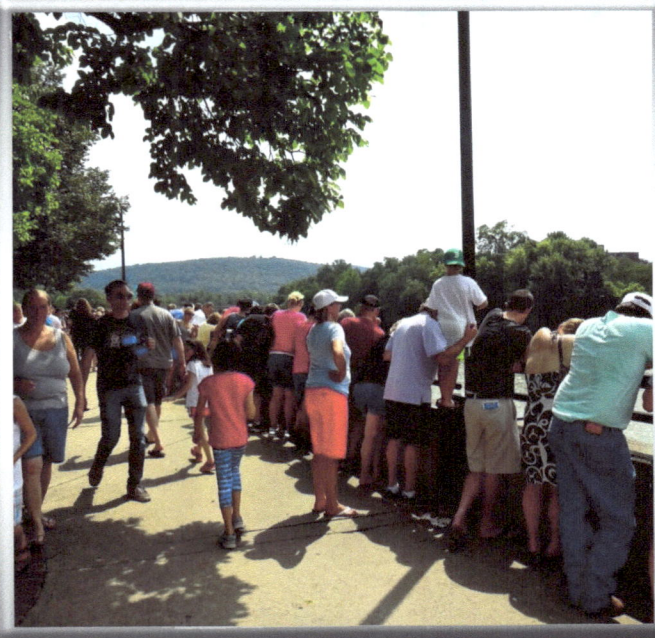

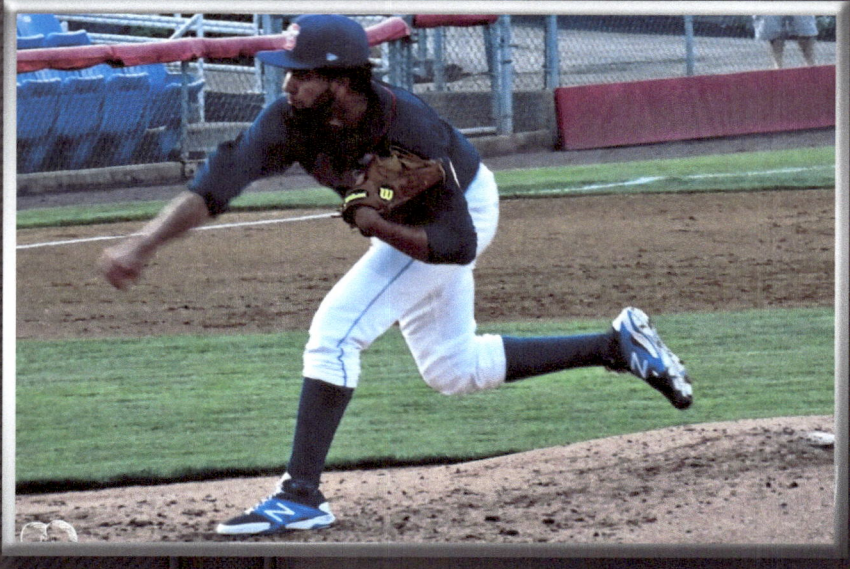
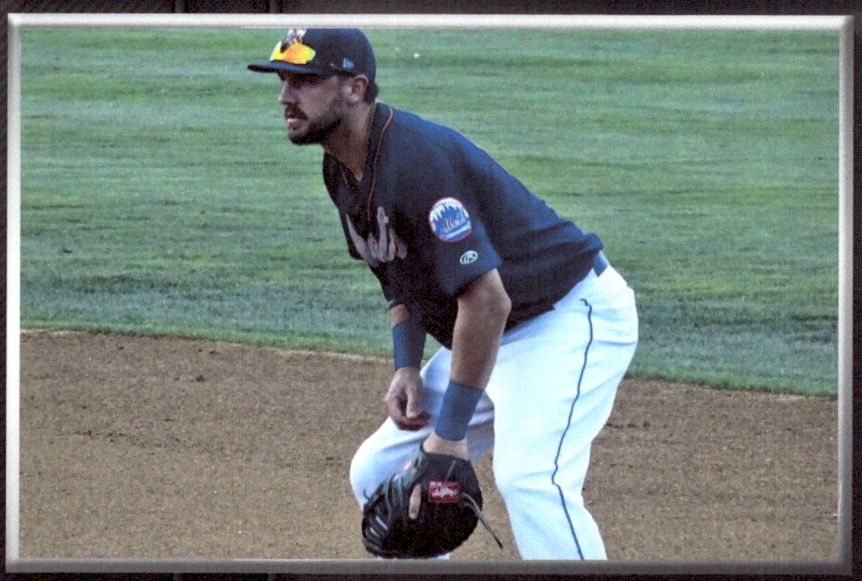

Binghamton Mets

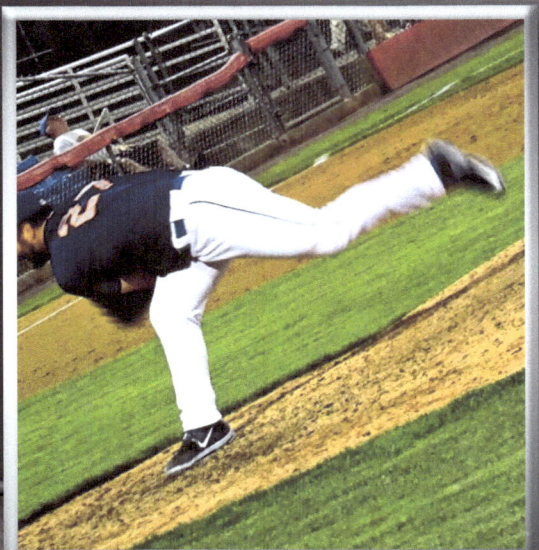
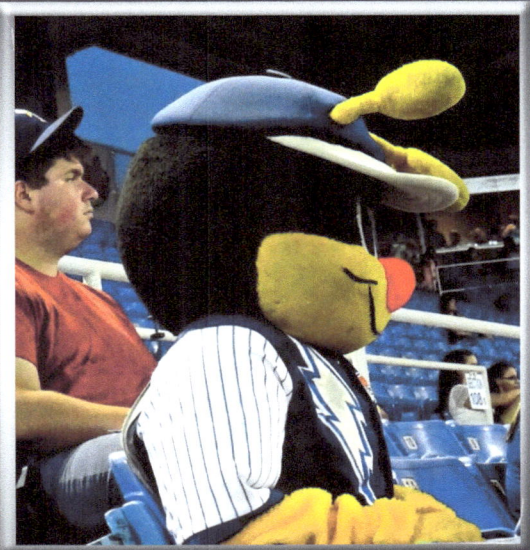
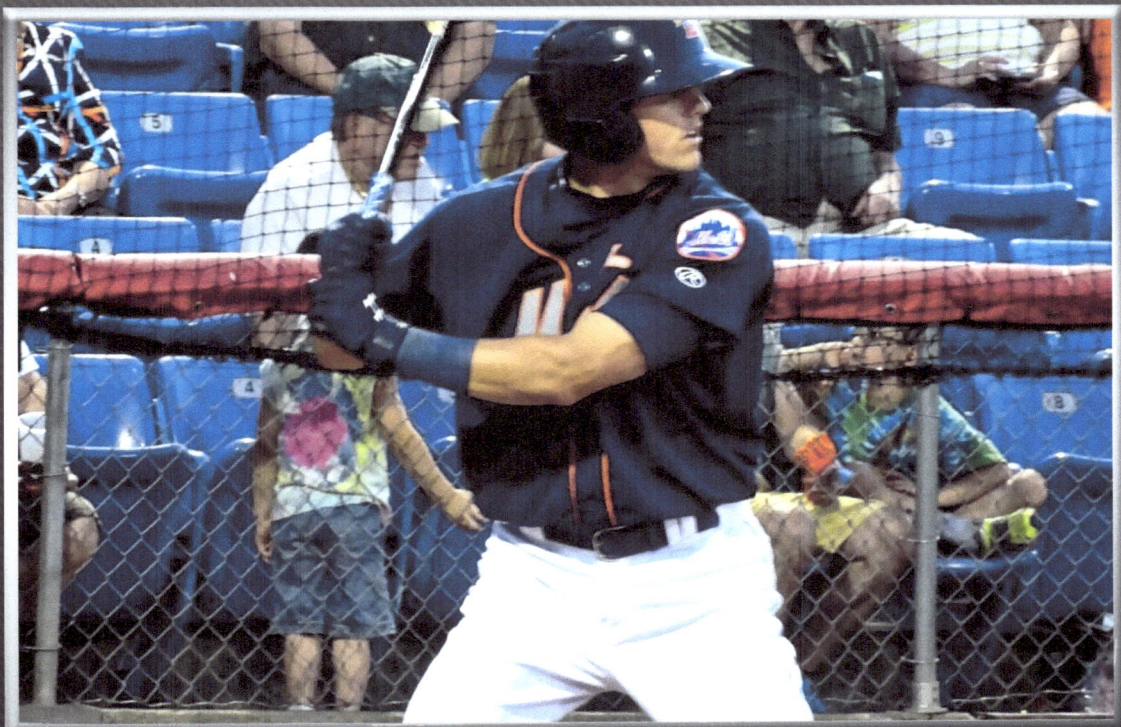

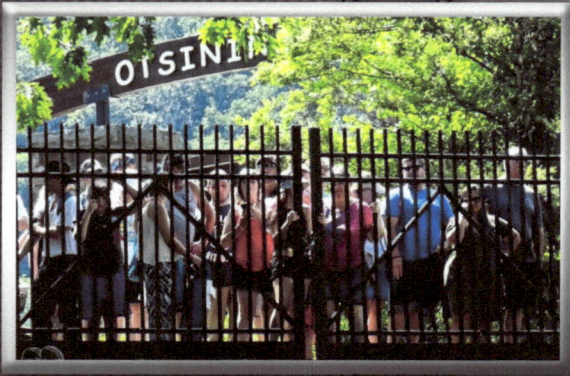
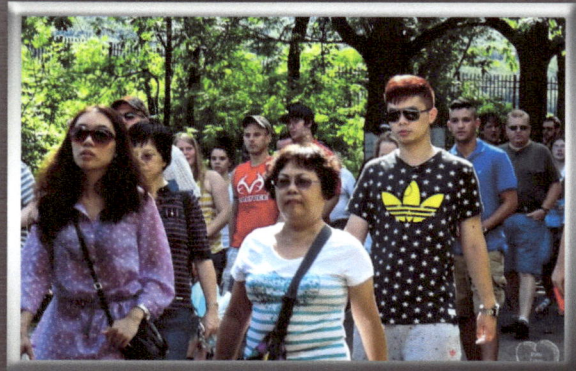
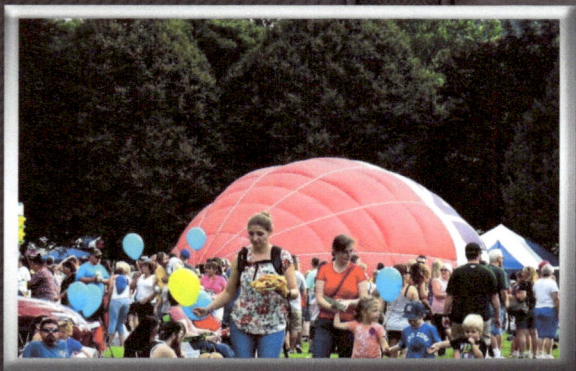
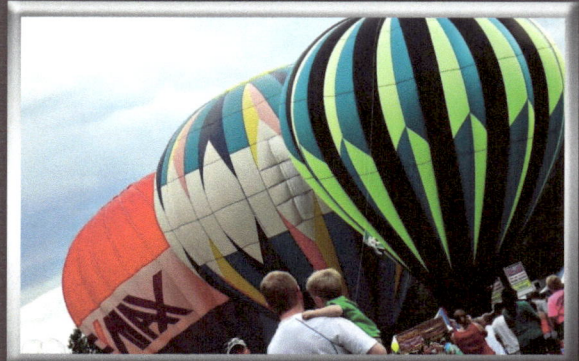
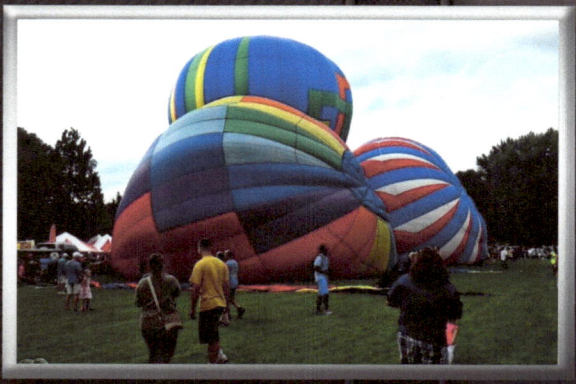
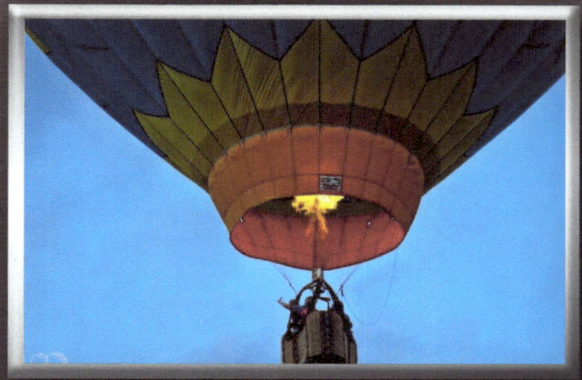

Spiedie Fest & Balloon Rally

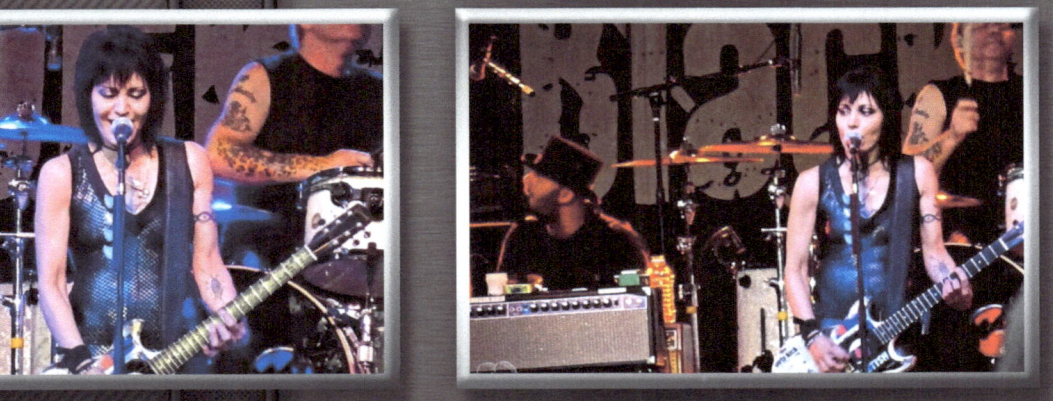
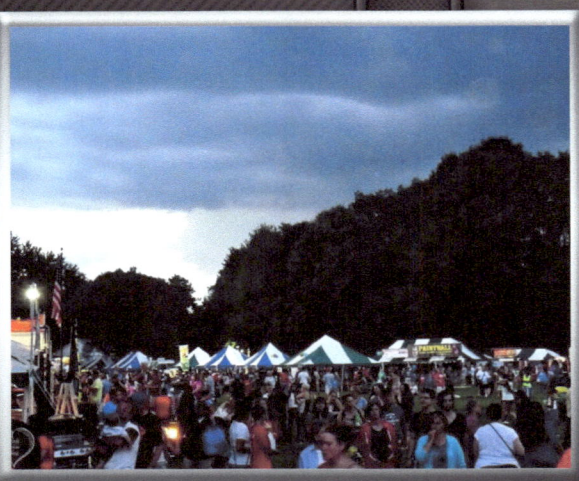
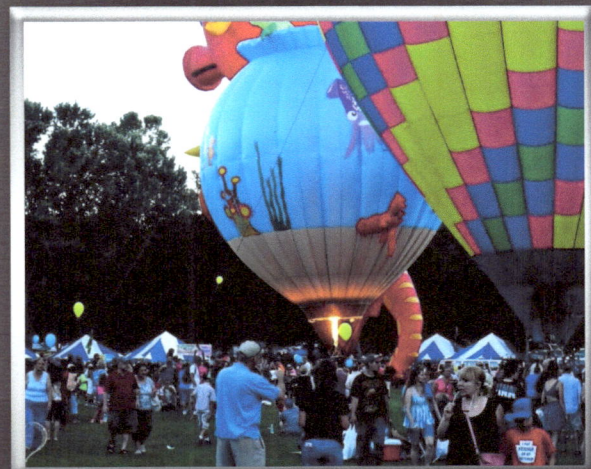
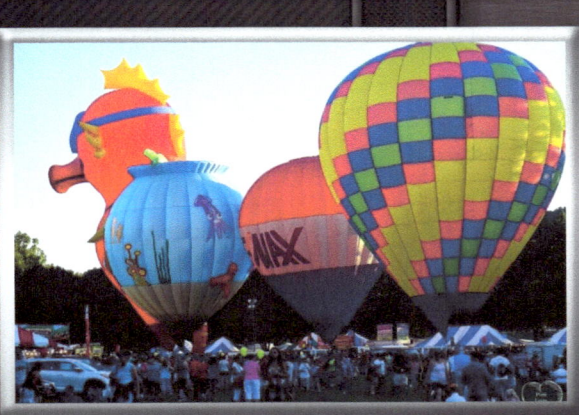
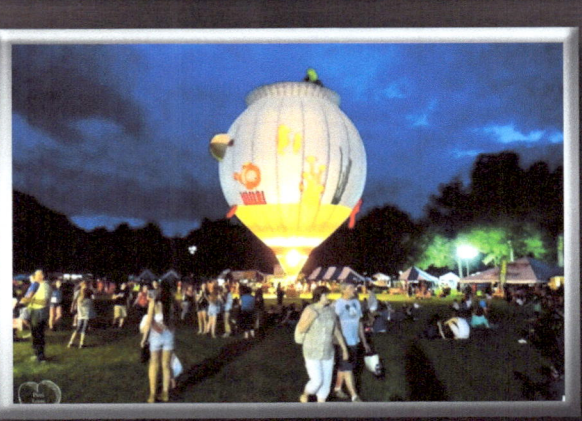

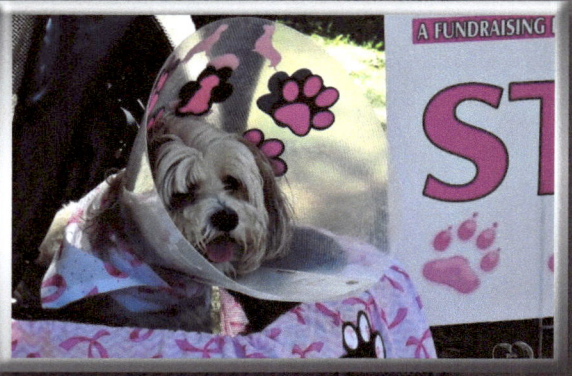
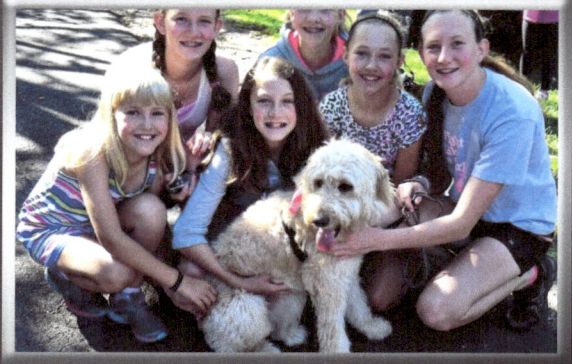
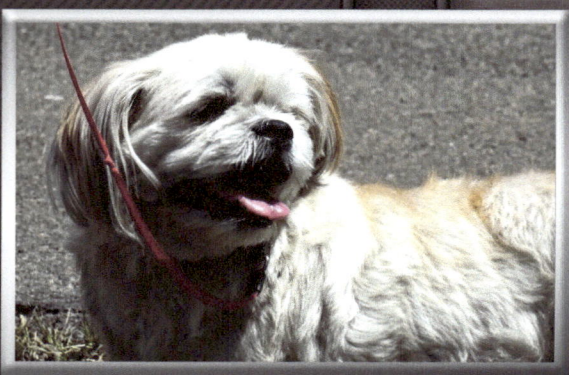
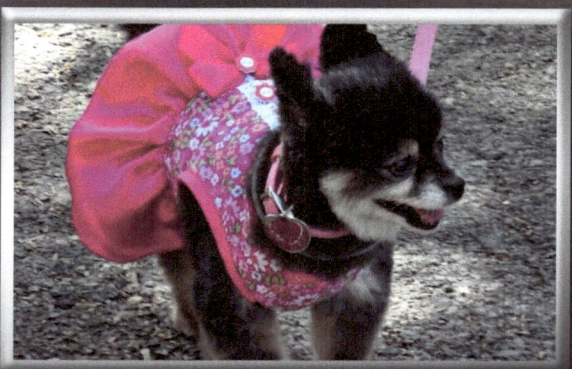
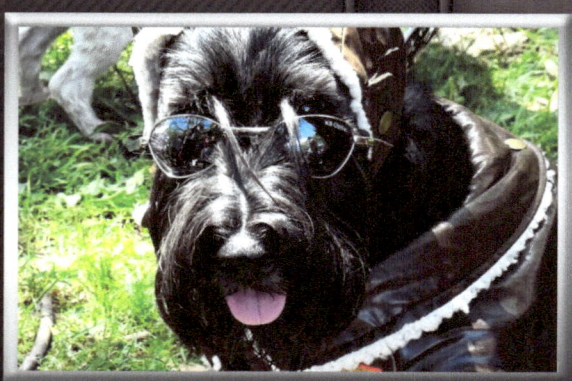
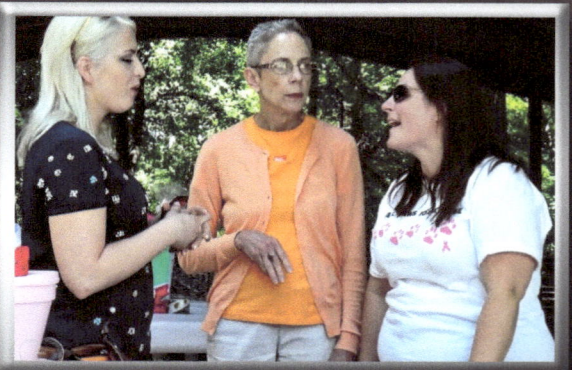

YWCA All Paws for a Cause

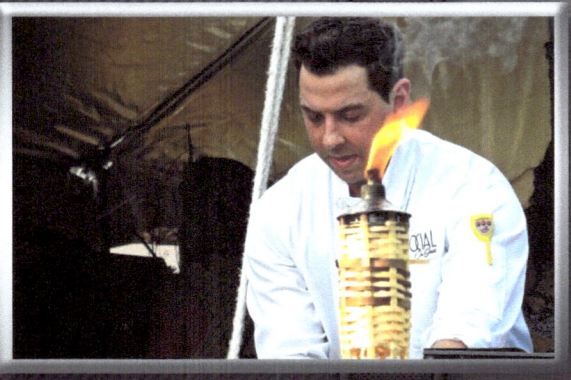
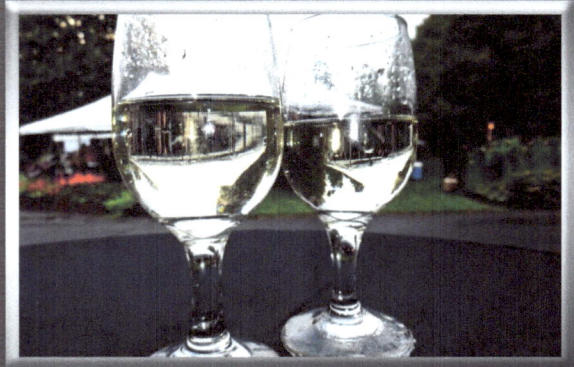
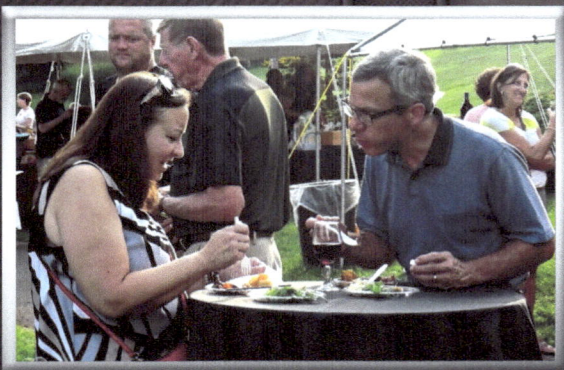
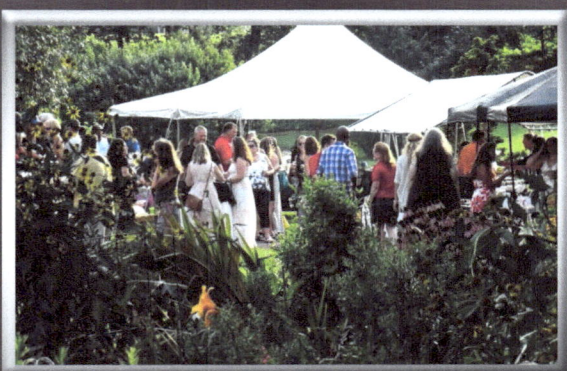
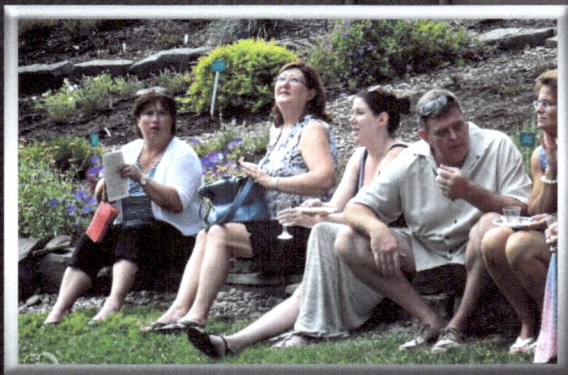
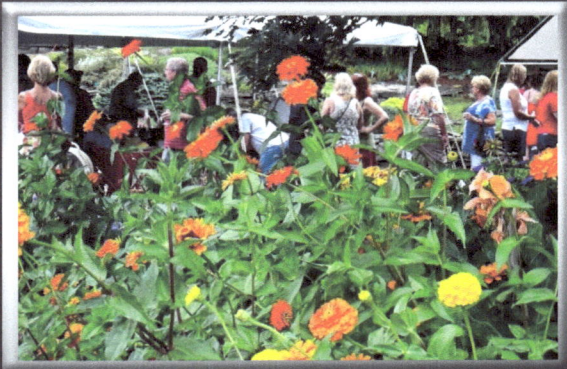

Fresh Food Face Off

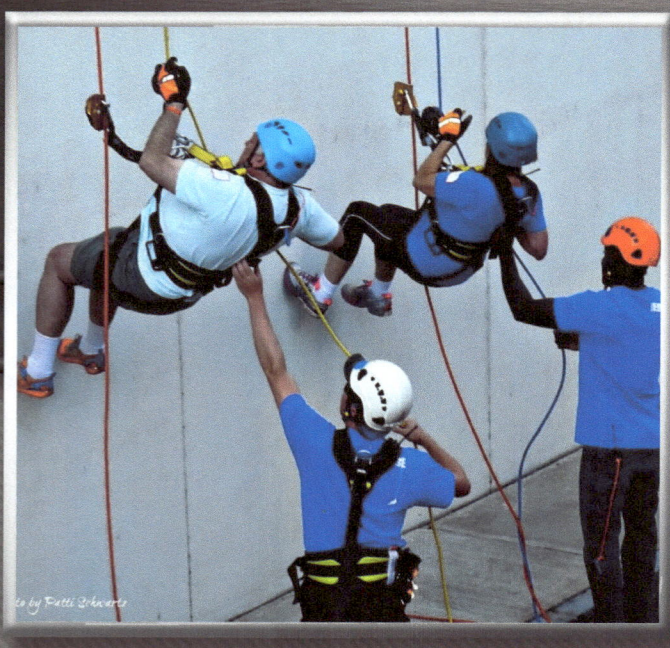
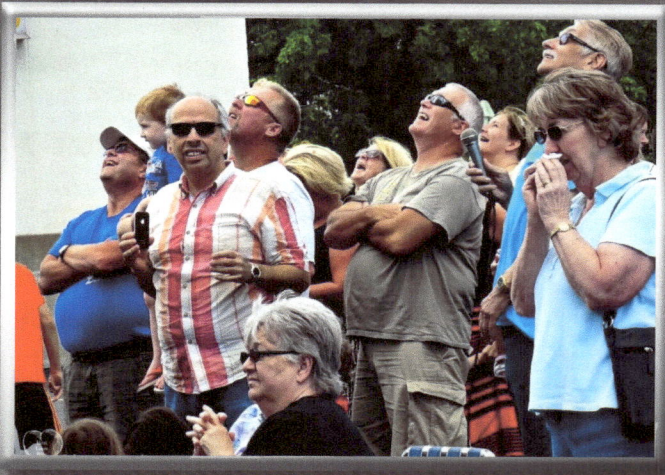
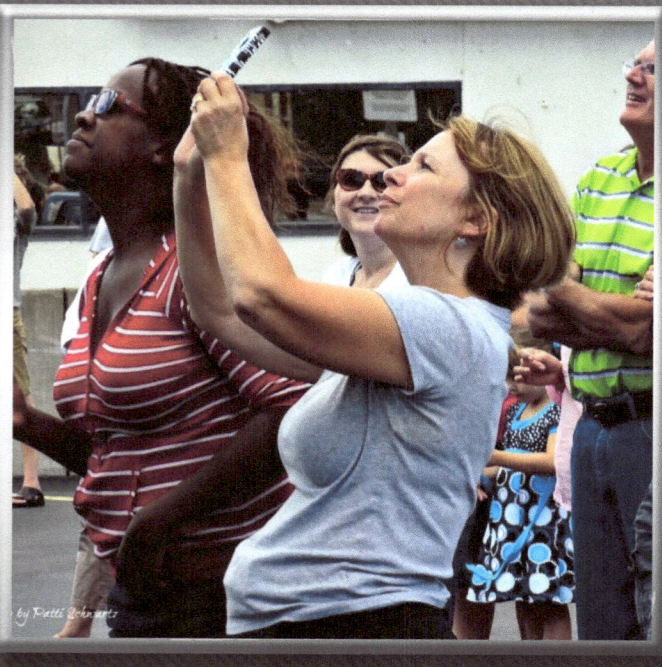
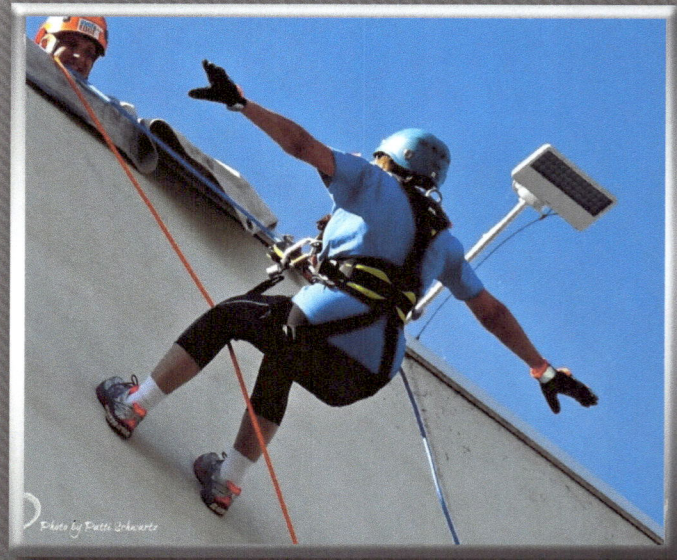

First Step for Catholic Charities

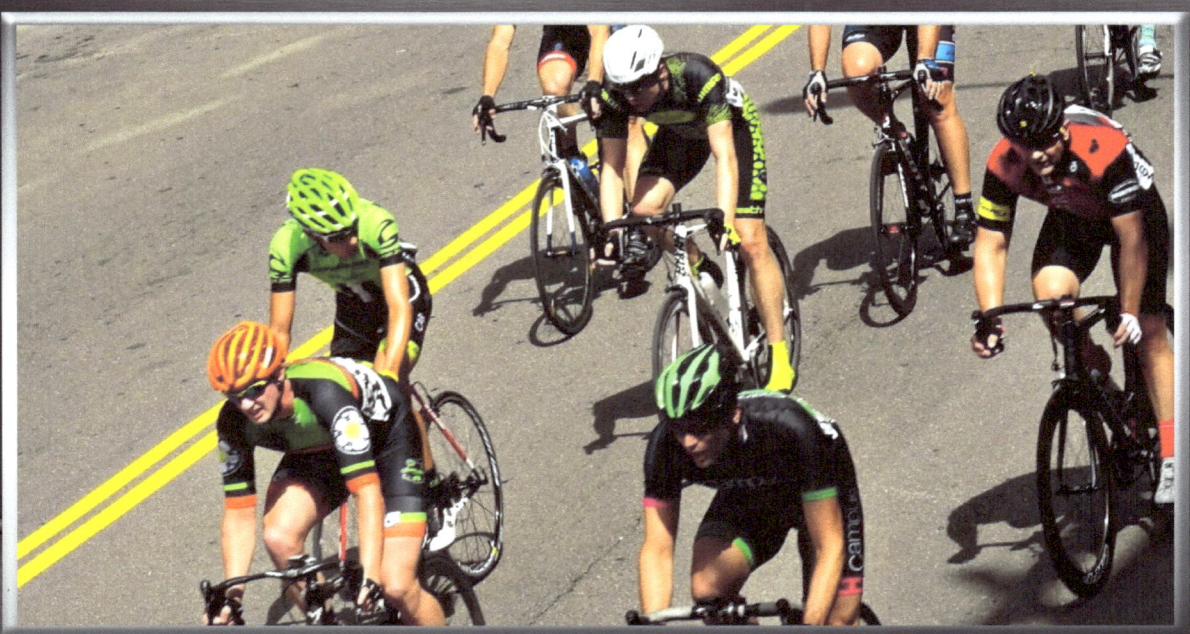

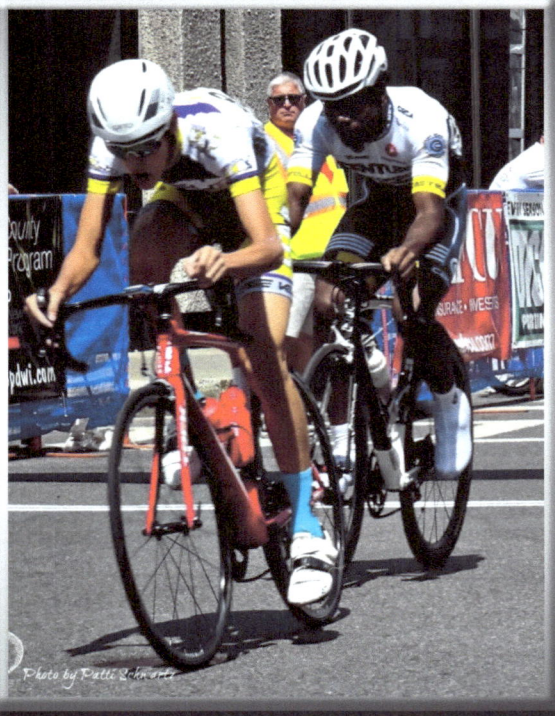

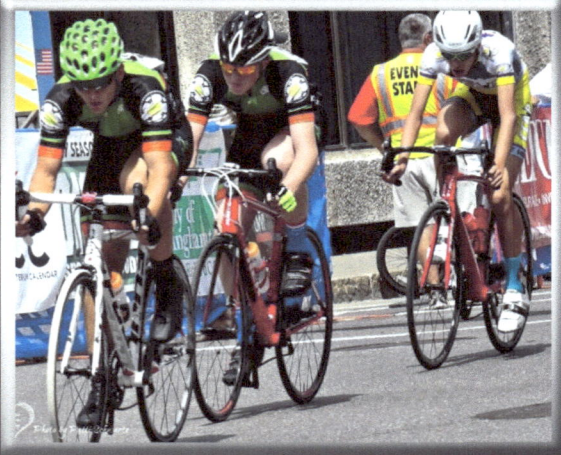

Chris Thater Races

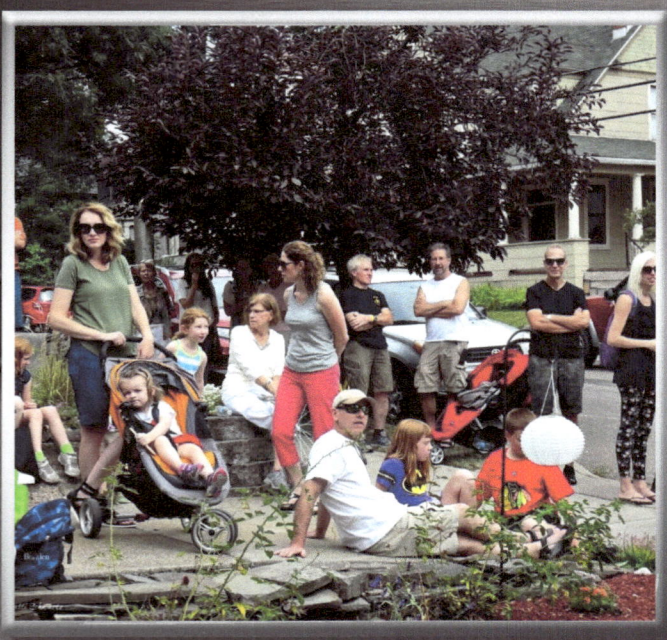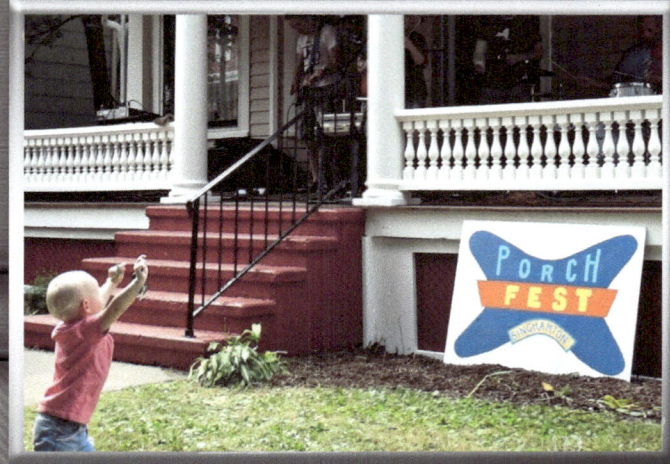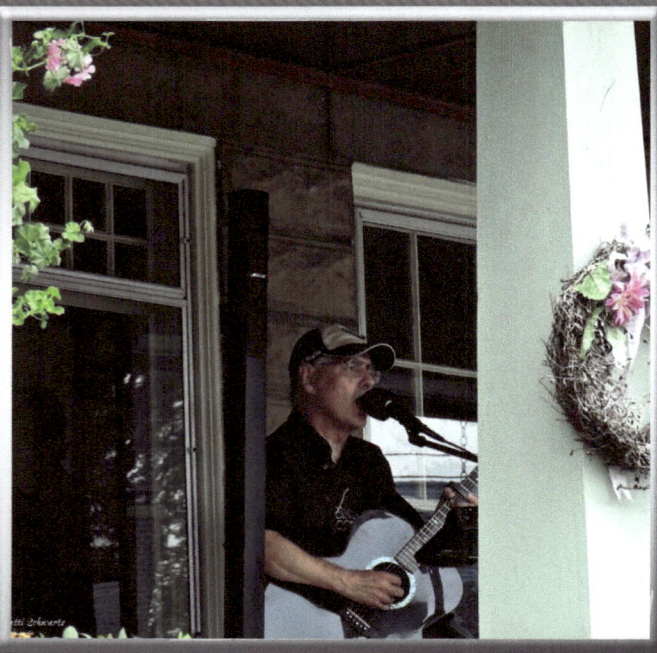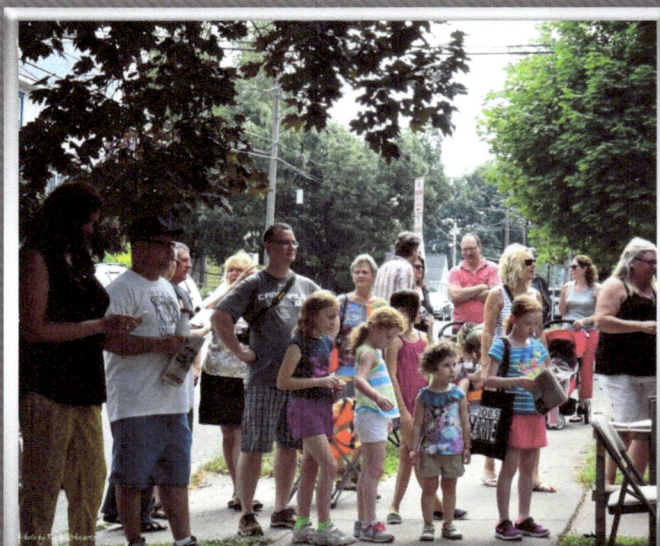

Binghamton Porch Fest

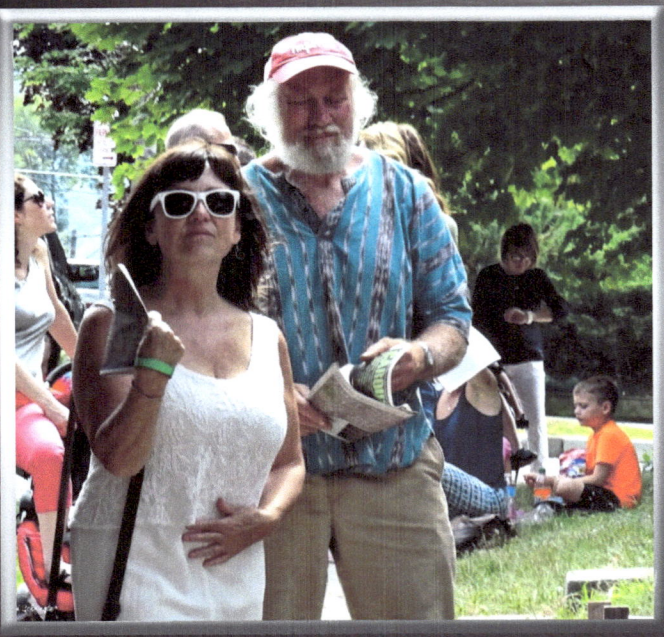
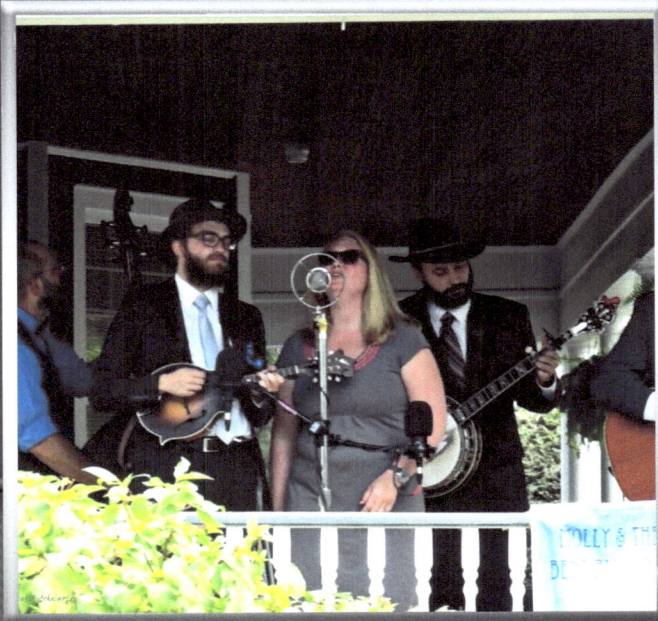
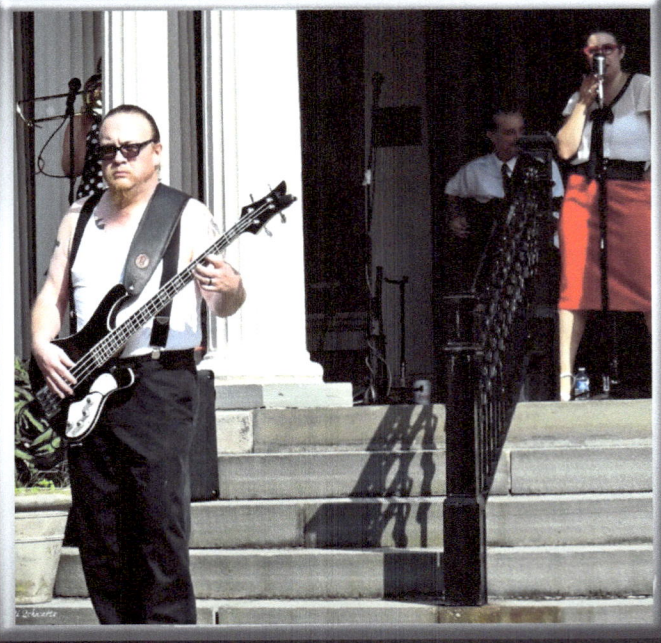
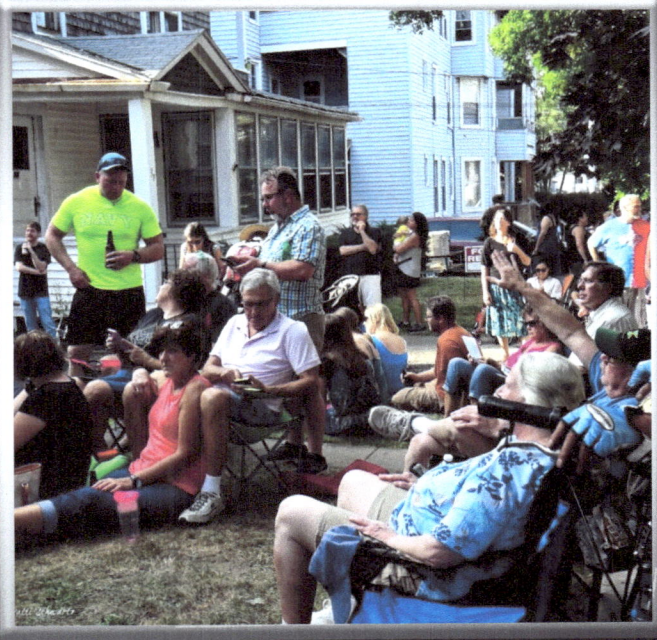

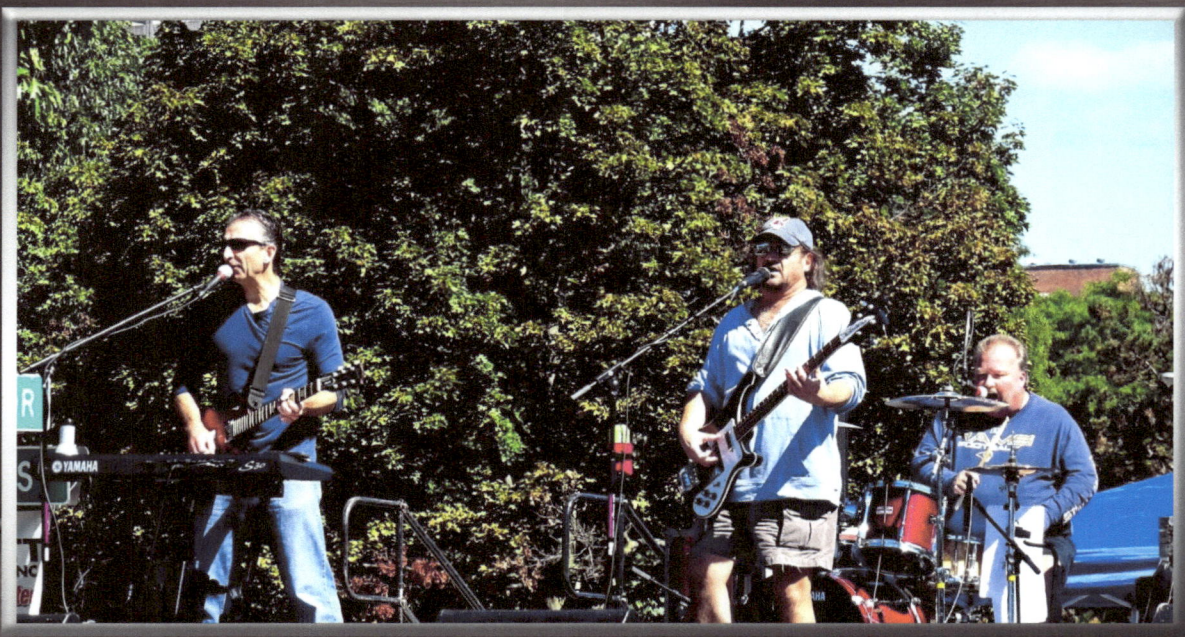
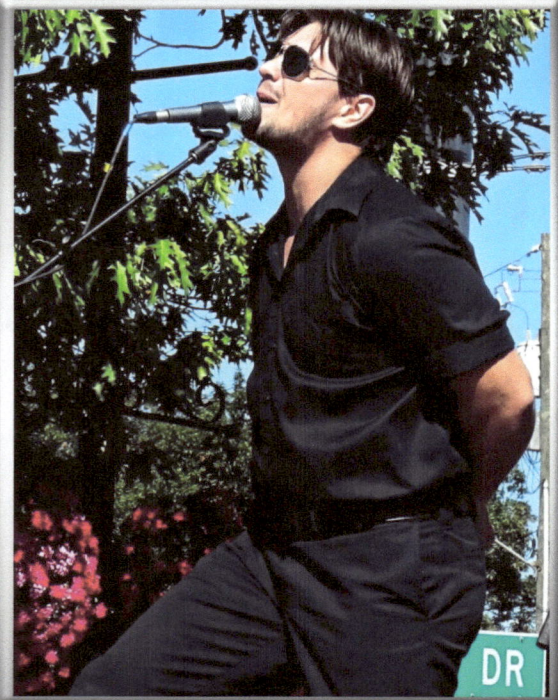
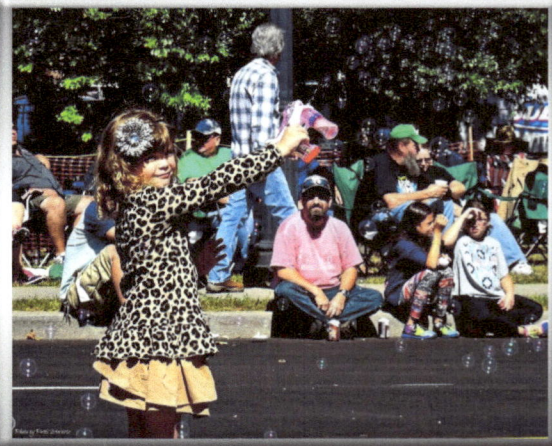

Blues on the Bridge

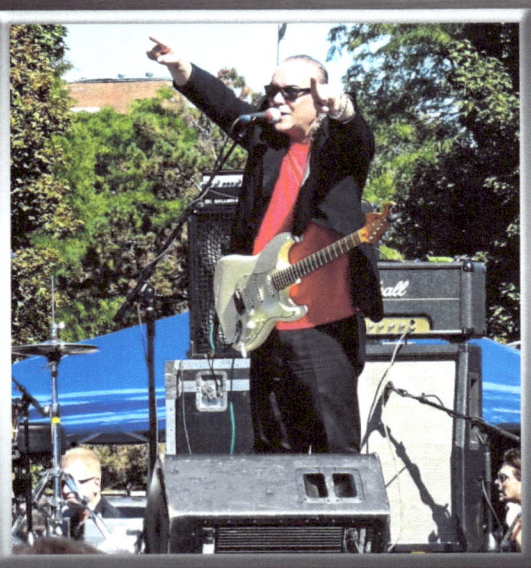
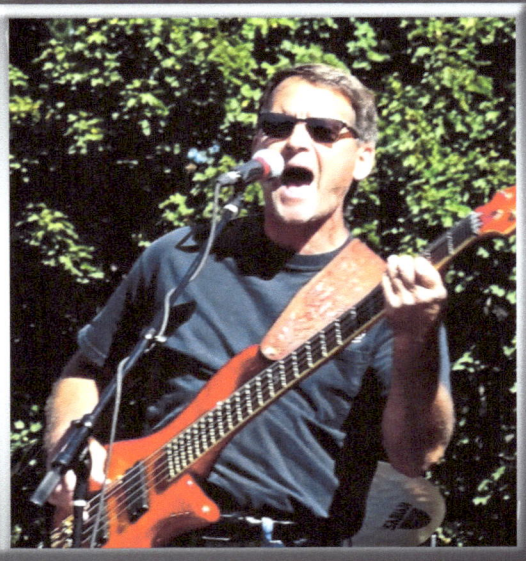
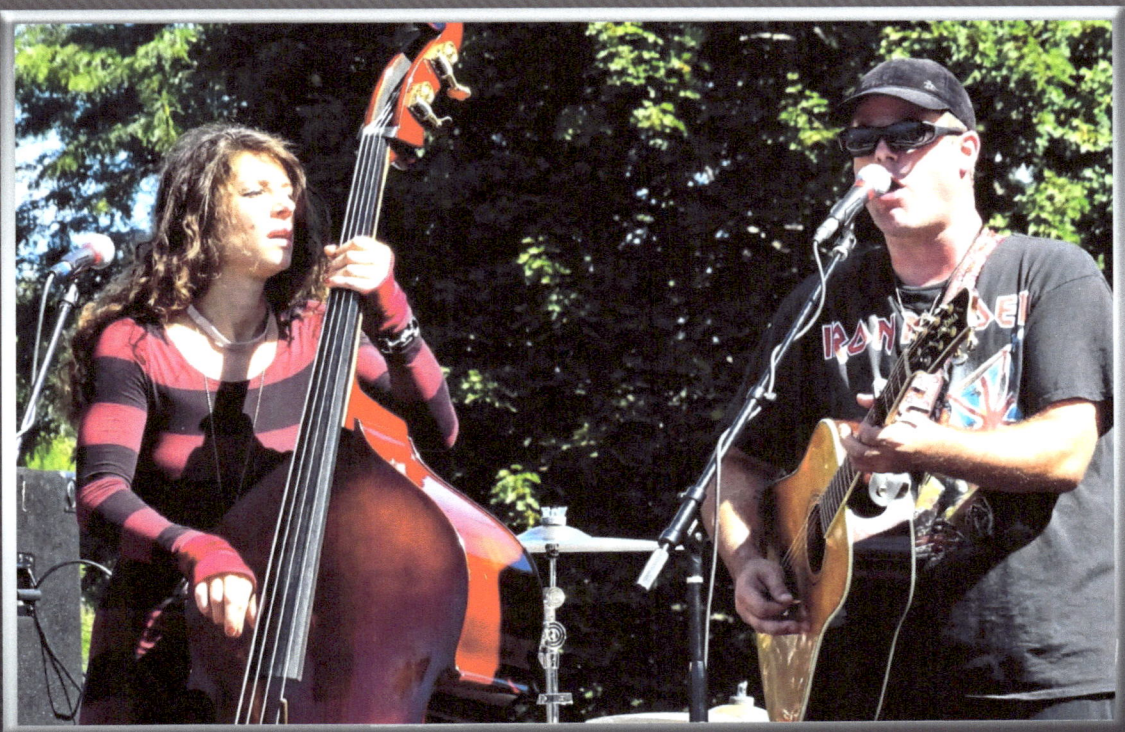

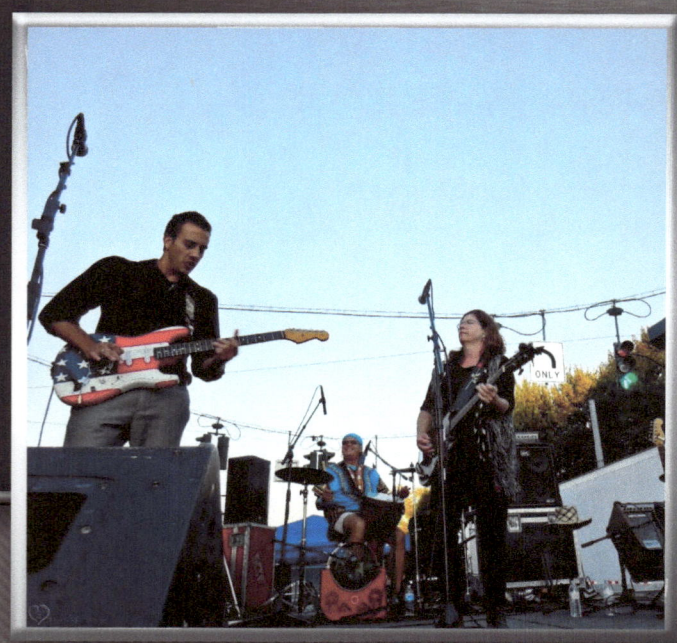
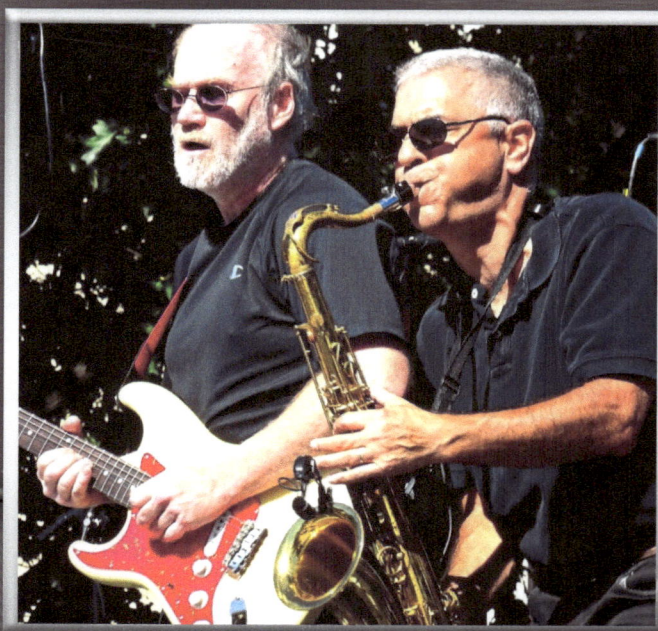
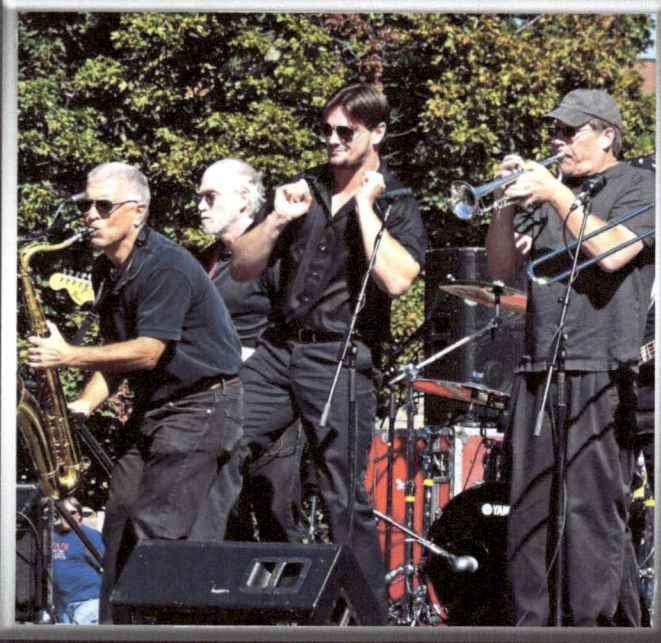
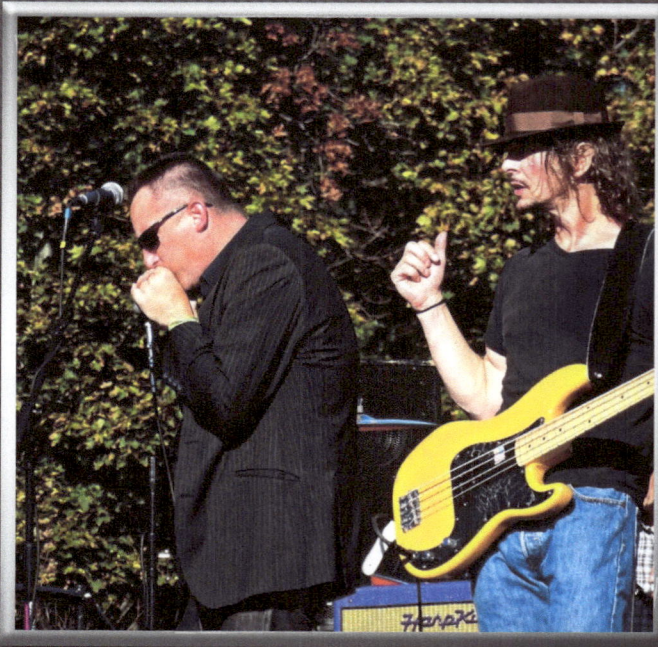

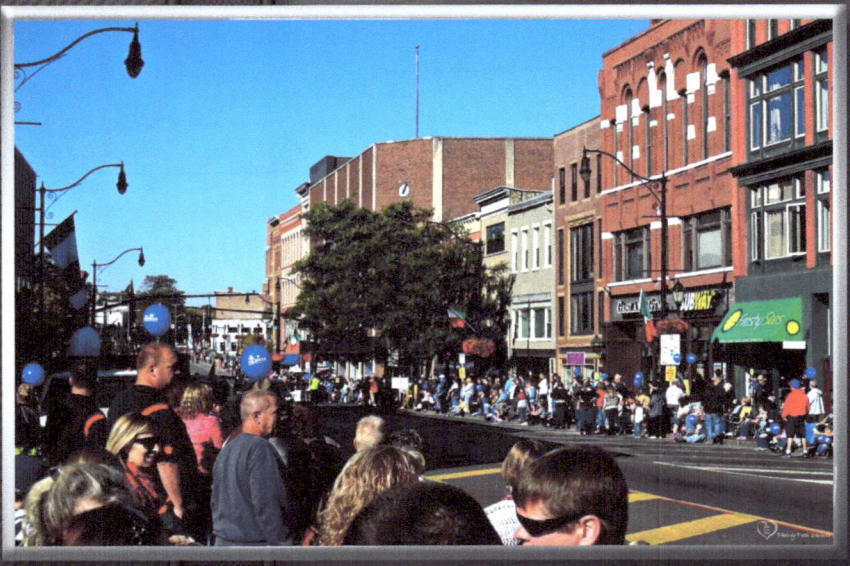
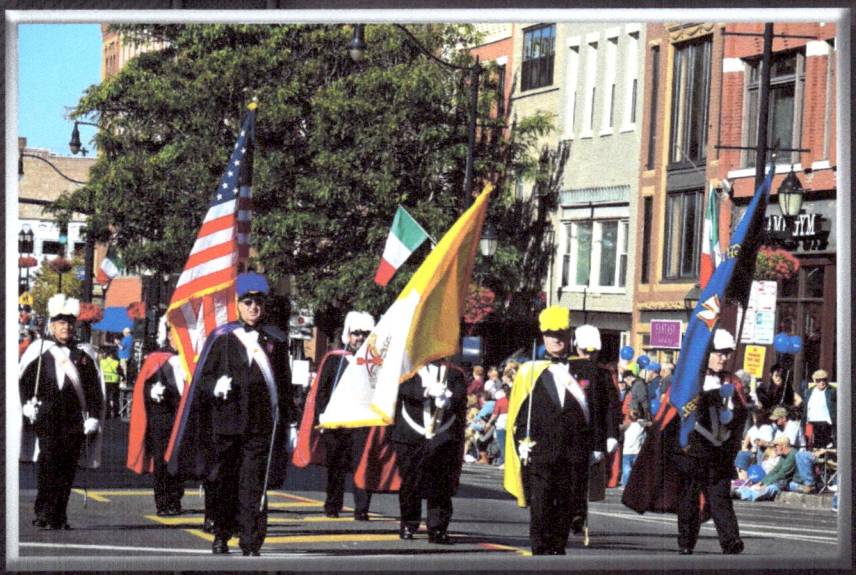

Columbus Day Parade

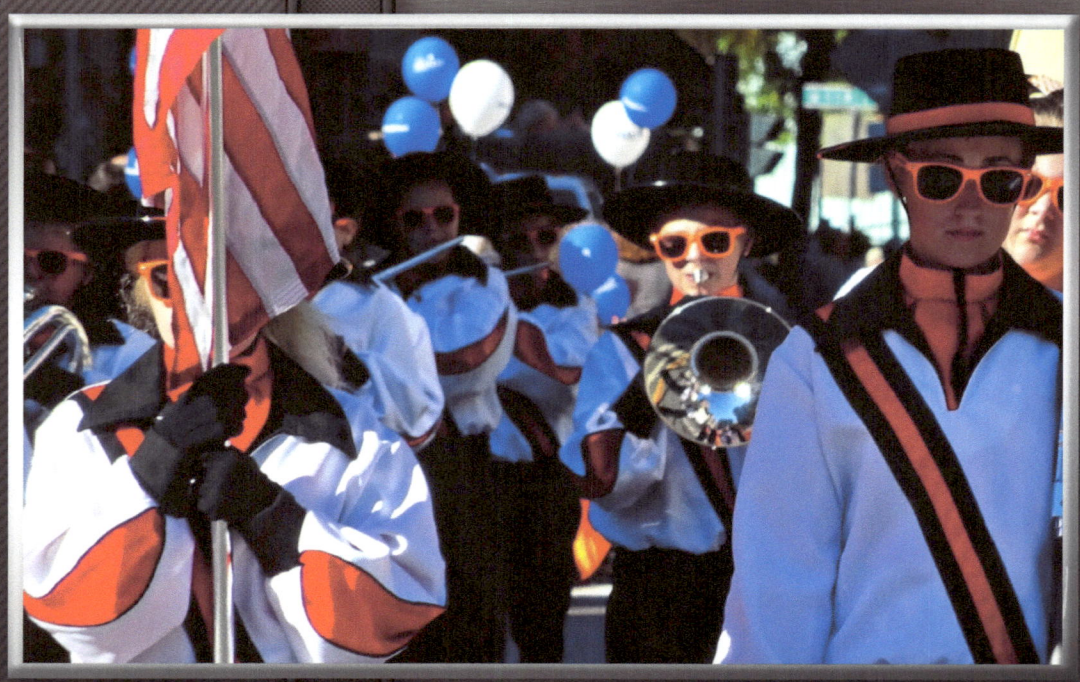
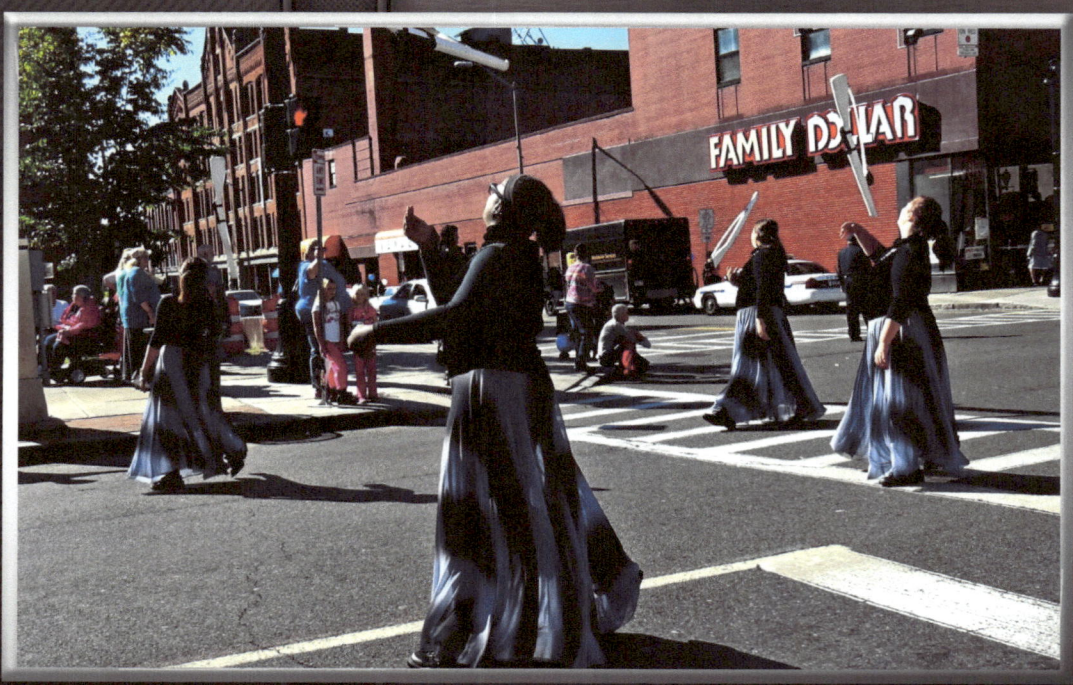

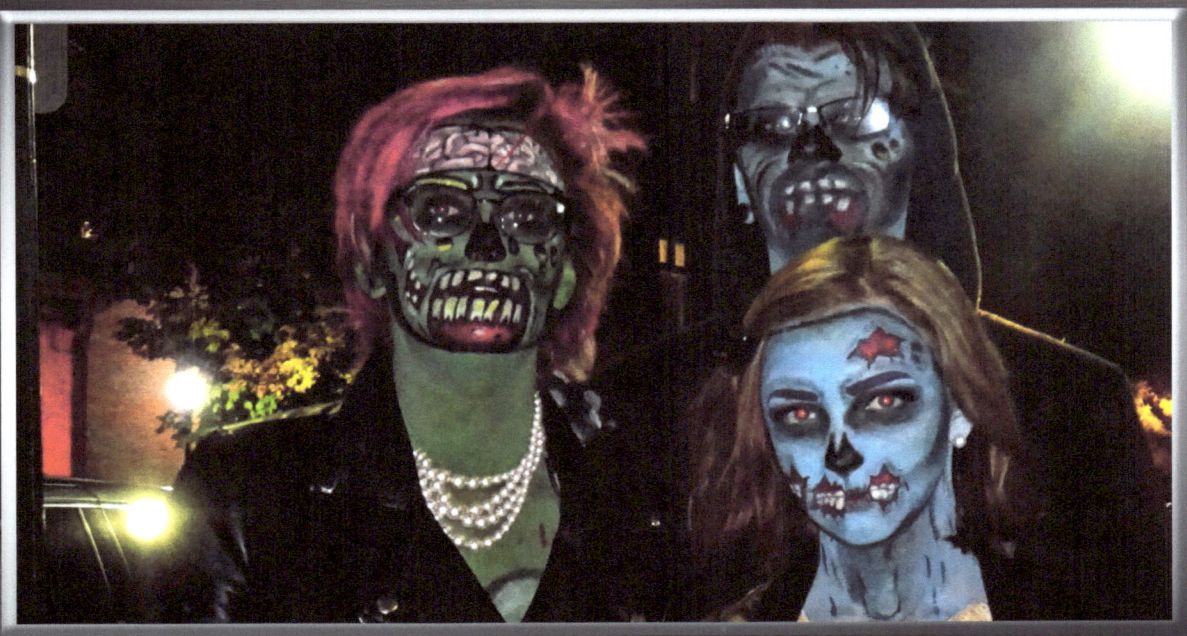
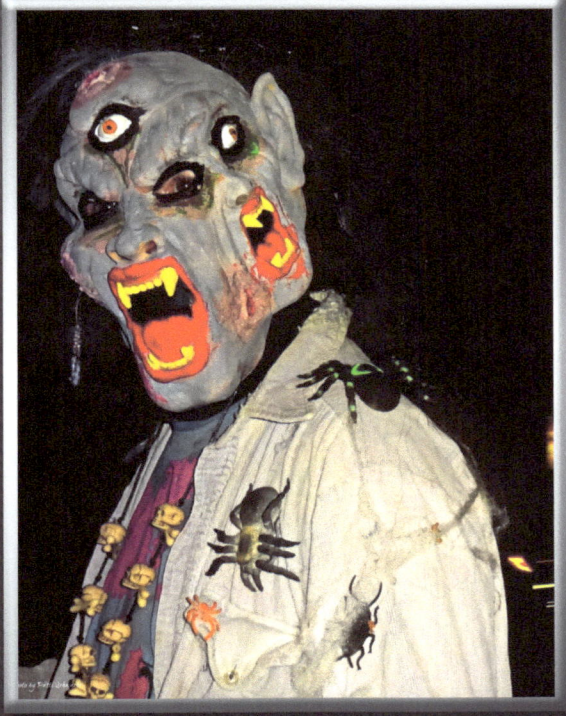
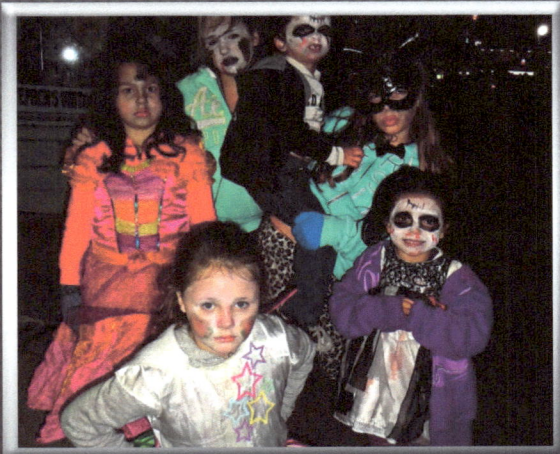

Annual Zombie Walk

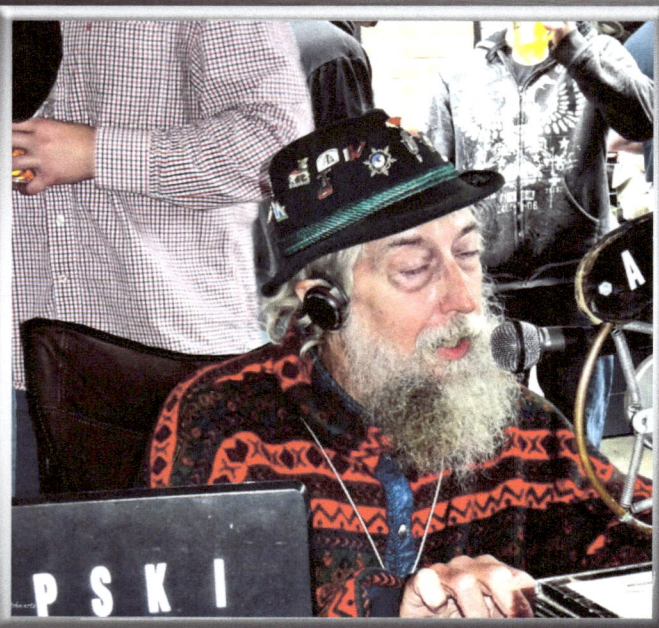
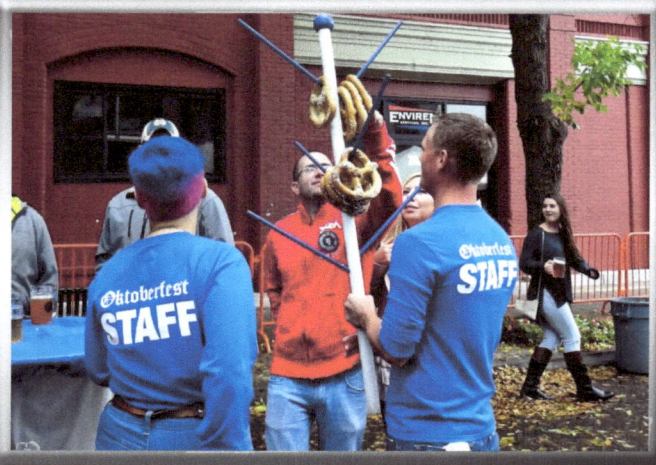
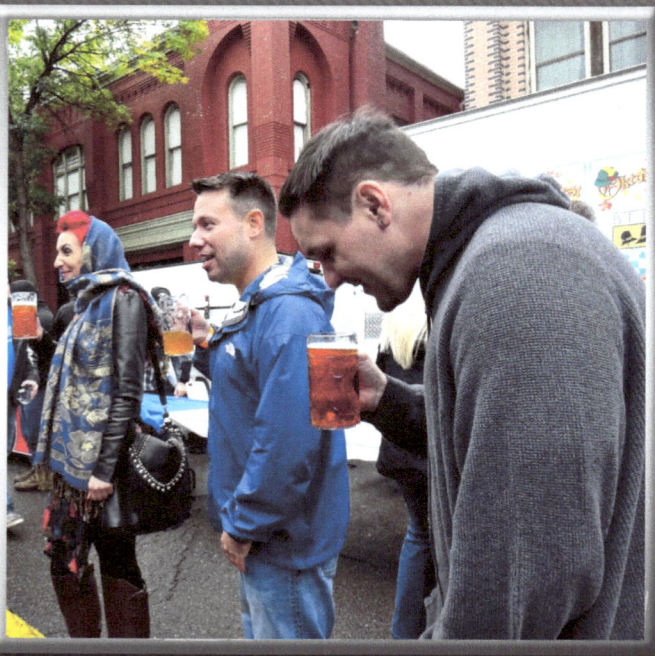
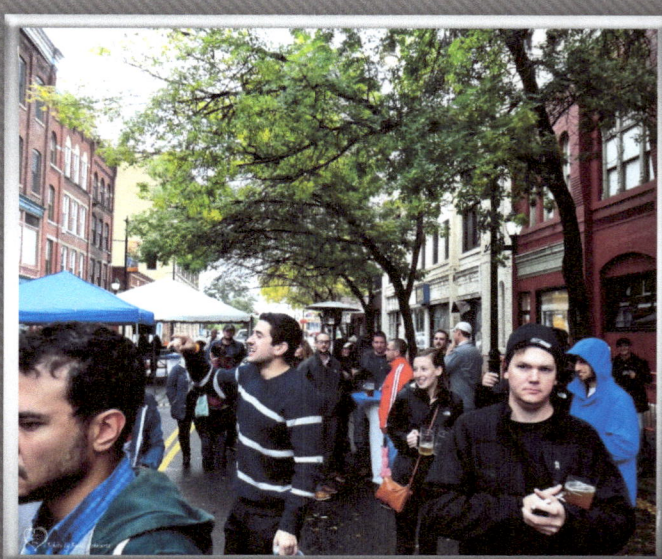

Oktoberfest

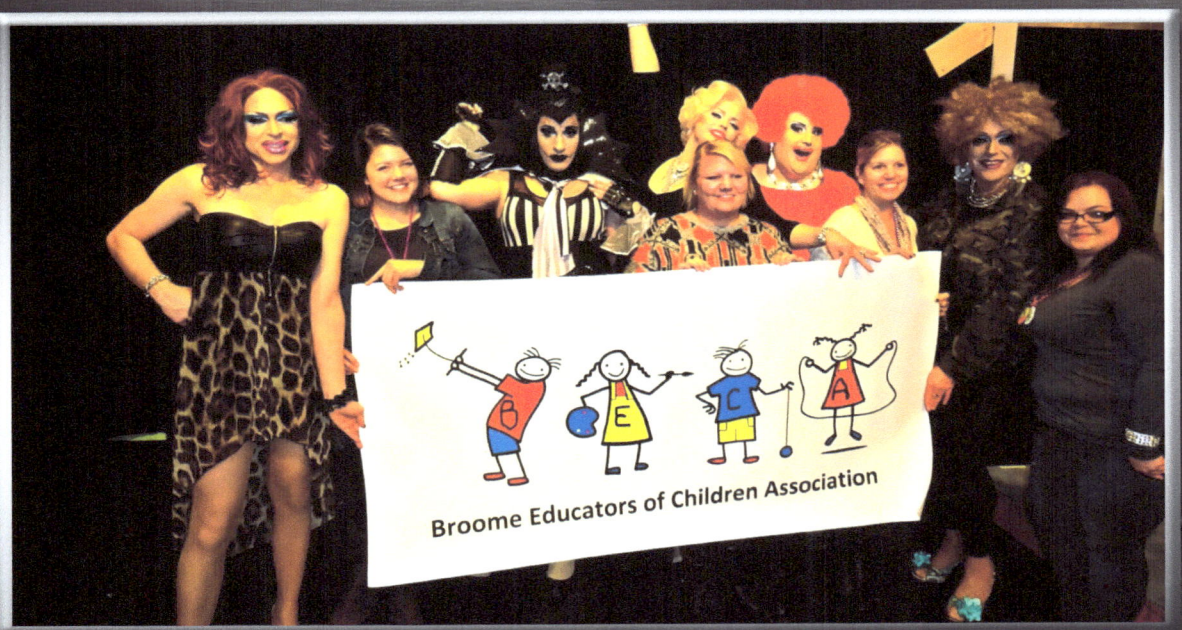
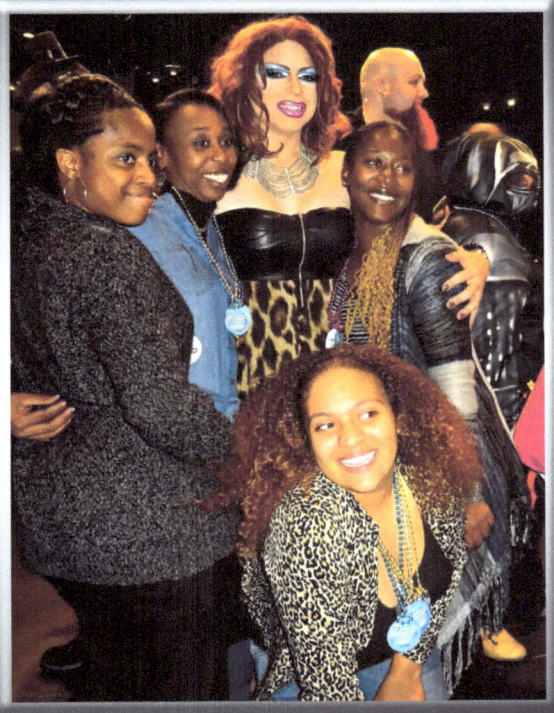
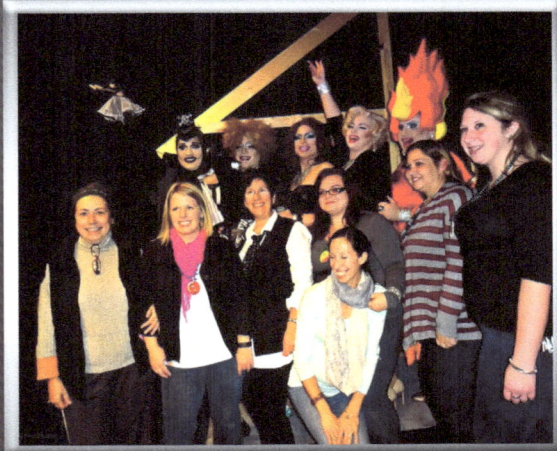

SUNY Broome Drag Show

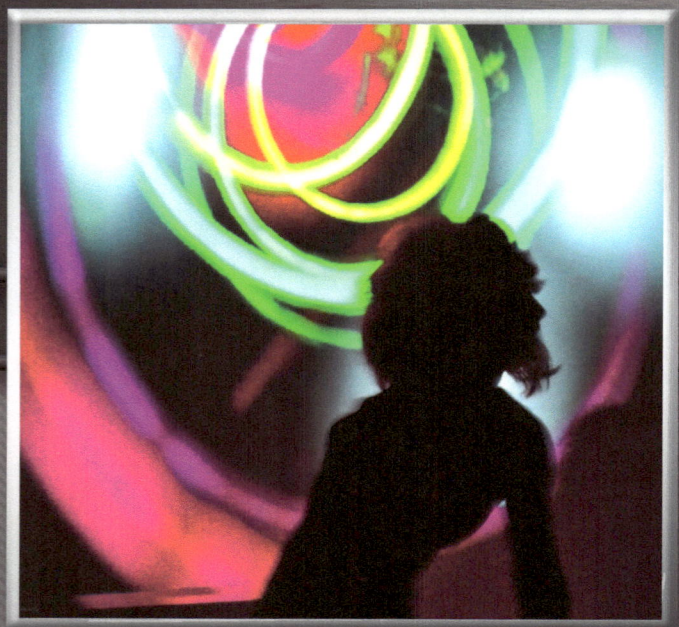
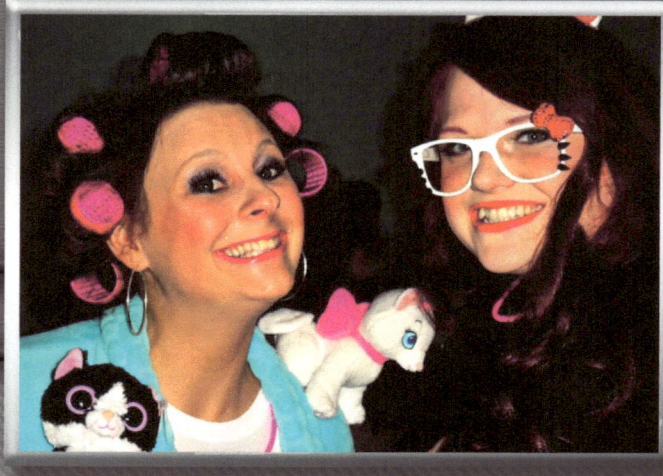
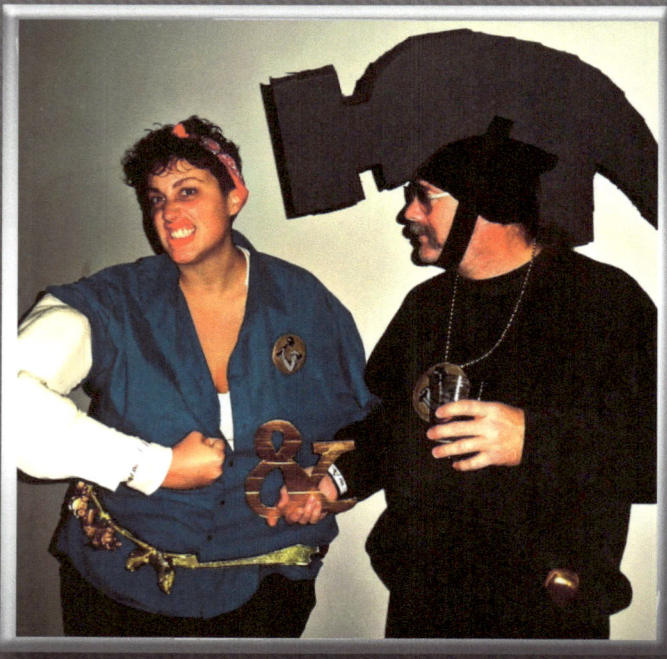
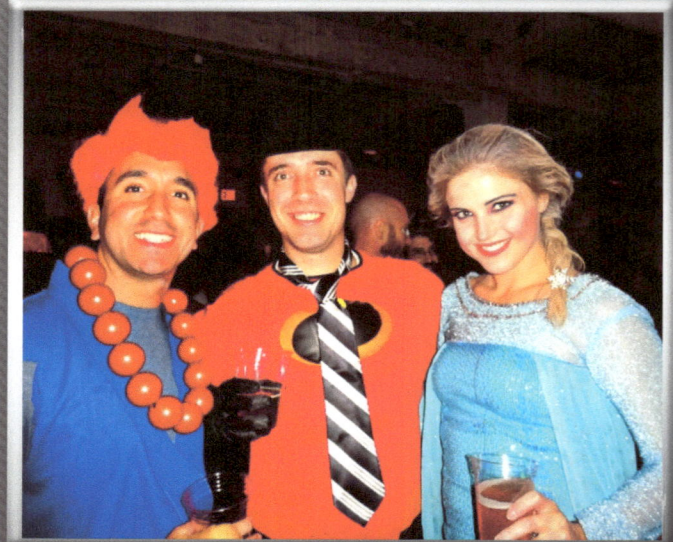

Triple Cities Scareousel Fantasmagorical Freakshow Ball

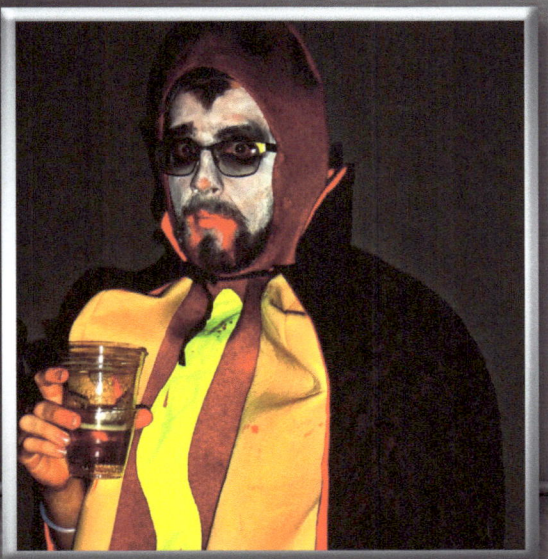
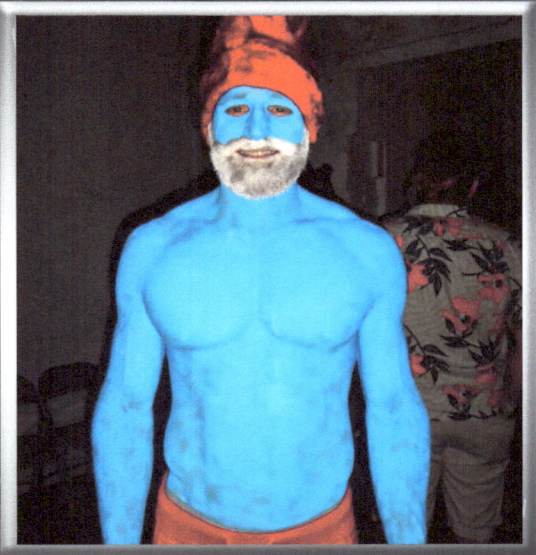
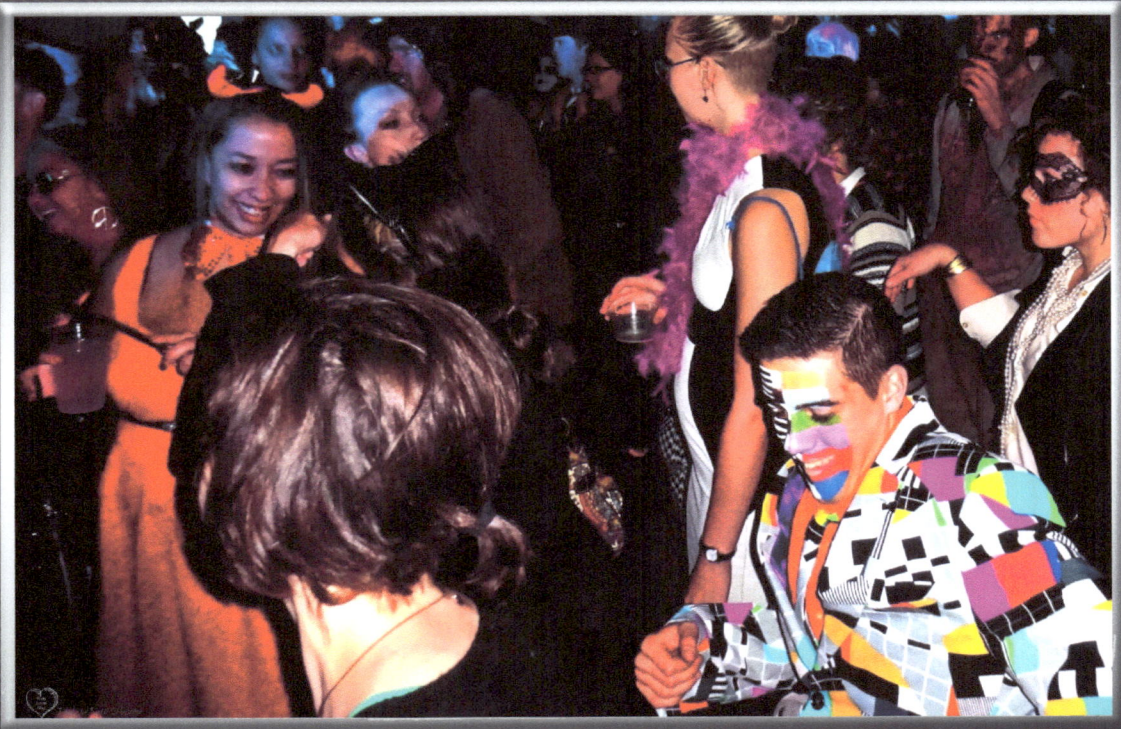

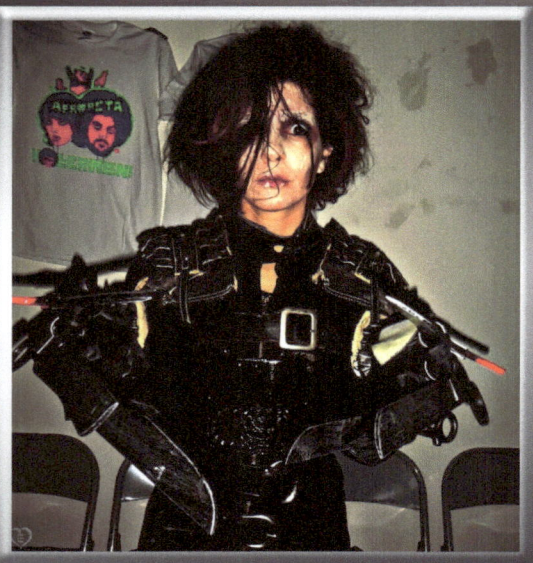
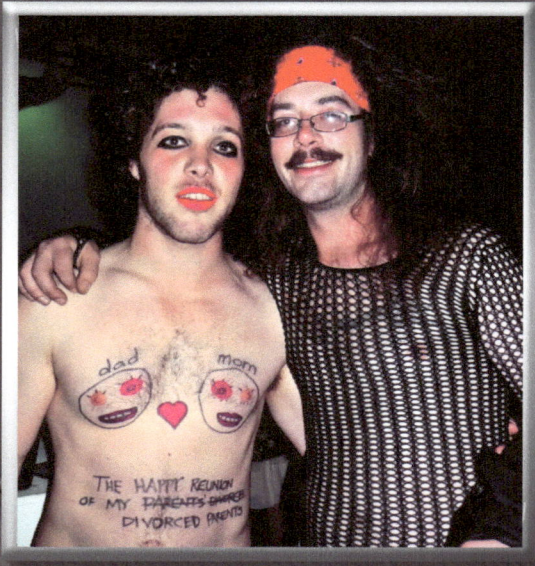
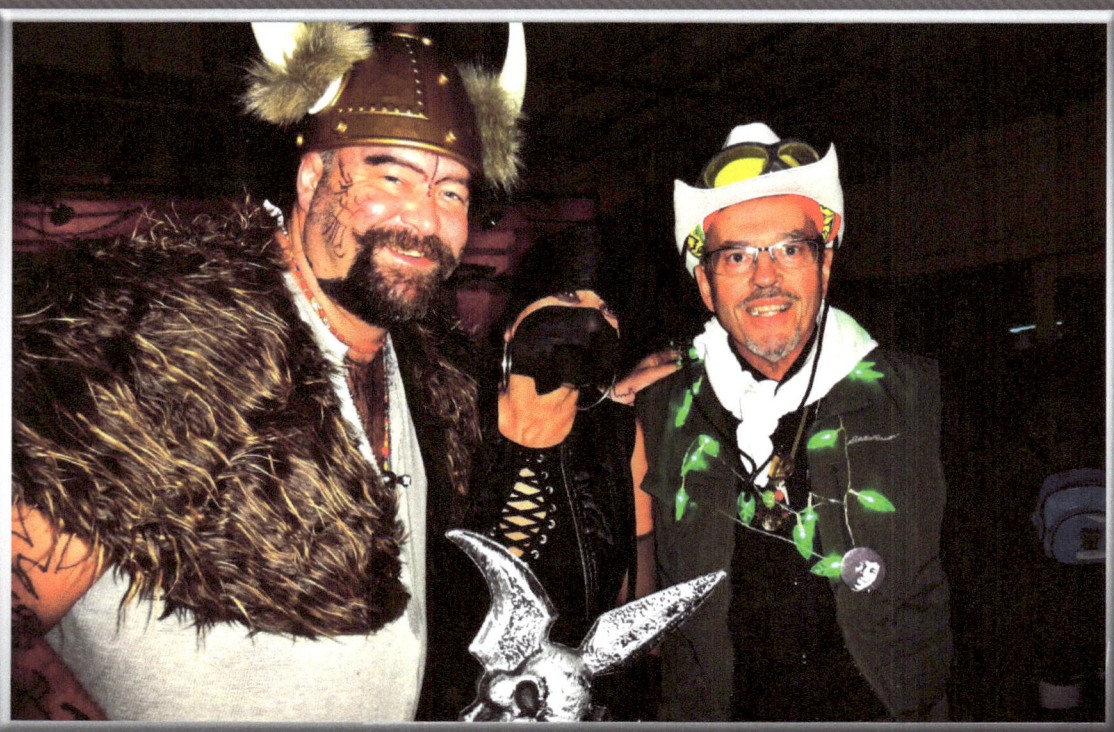

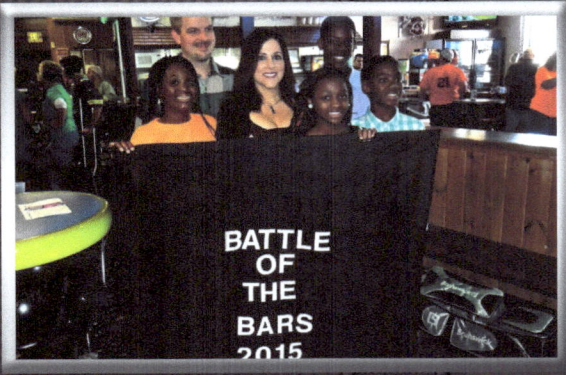
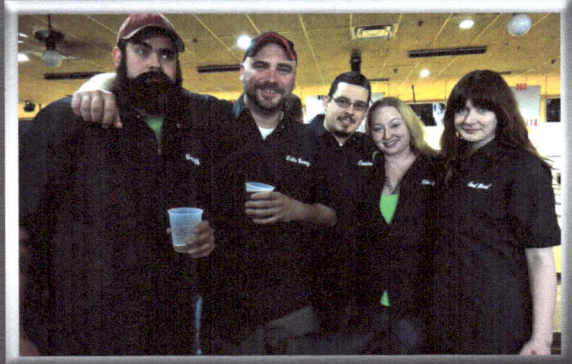
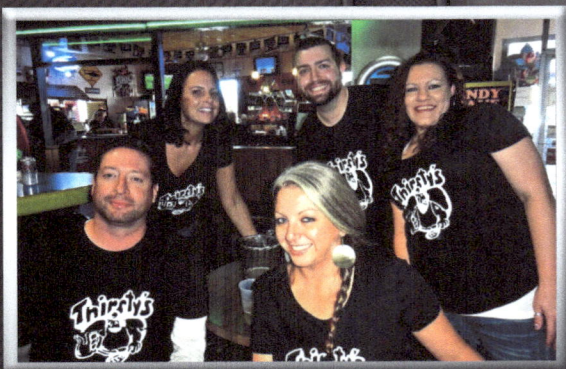
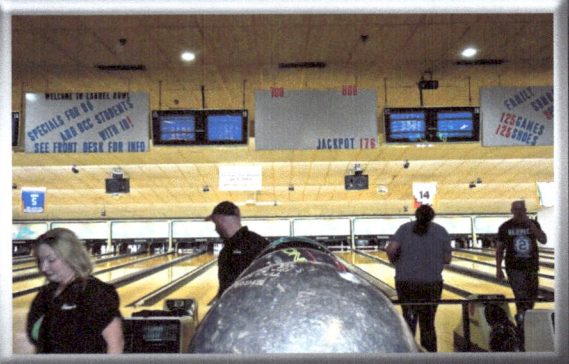
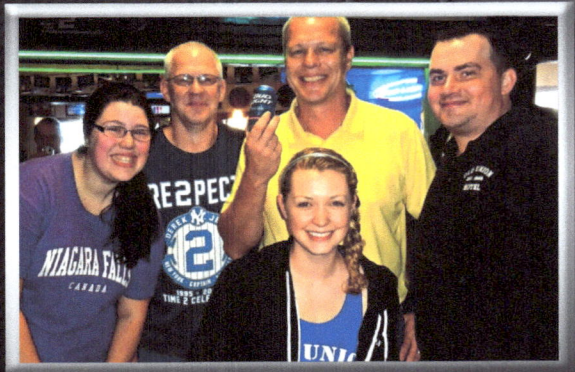
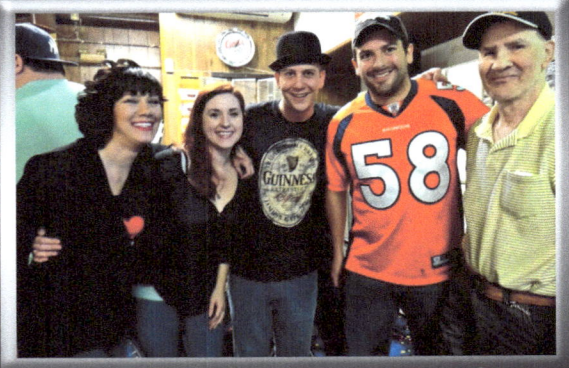

Battle of the Bars

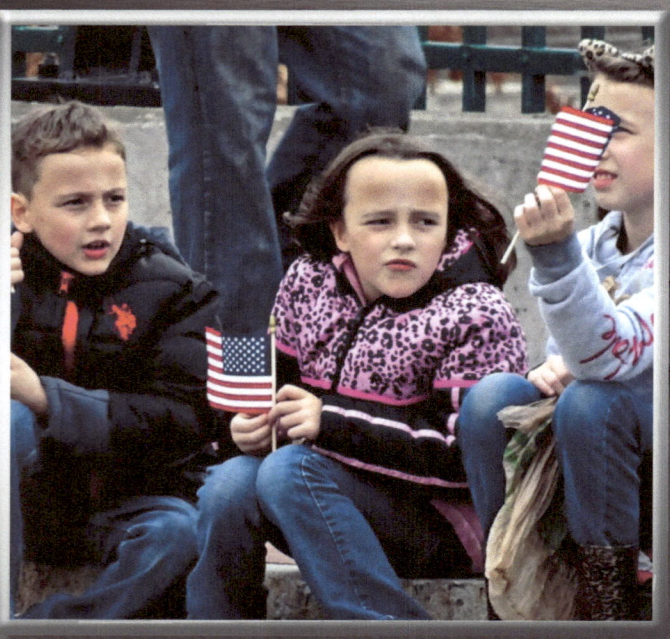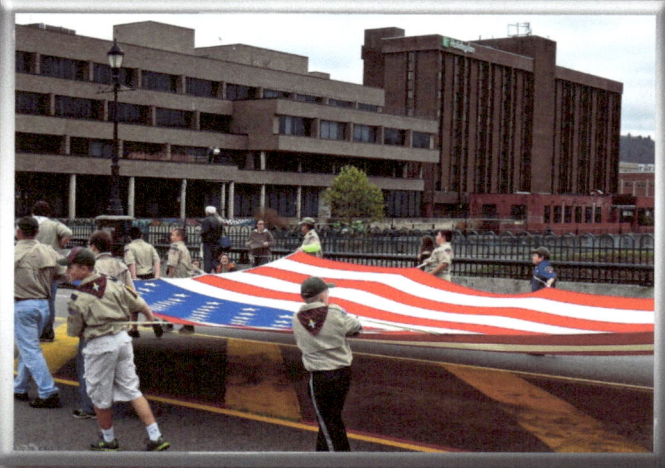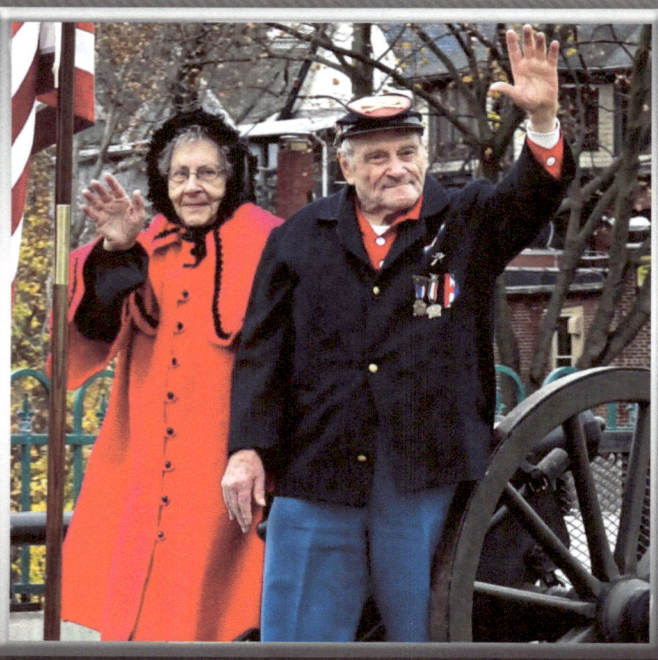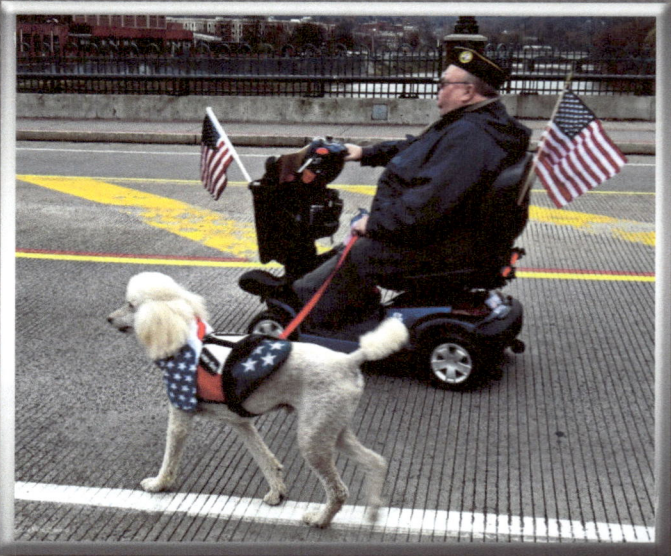

Veteran's Day Parade

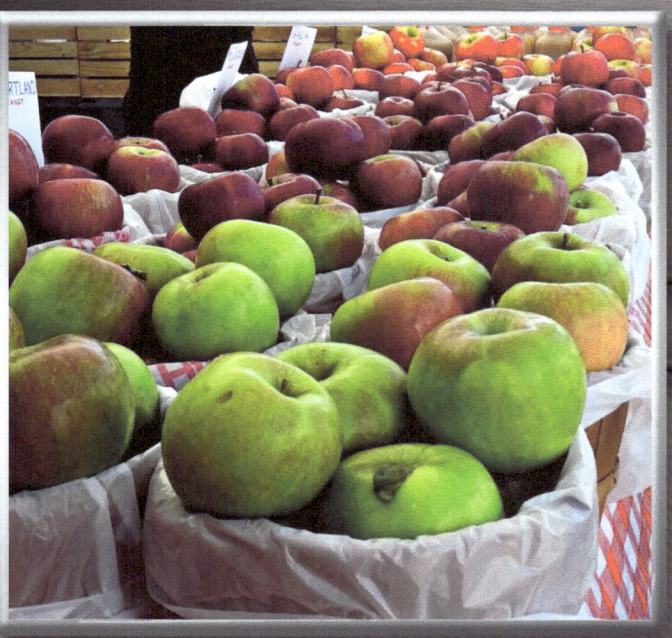
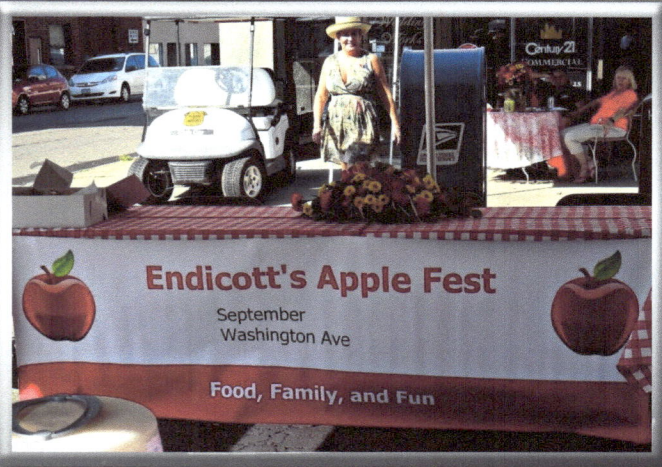
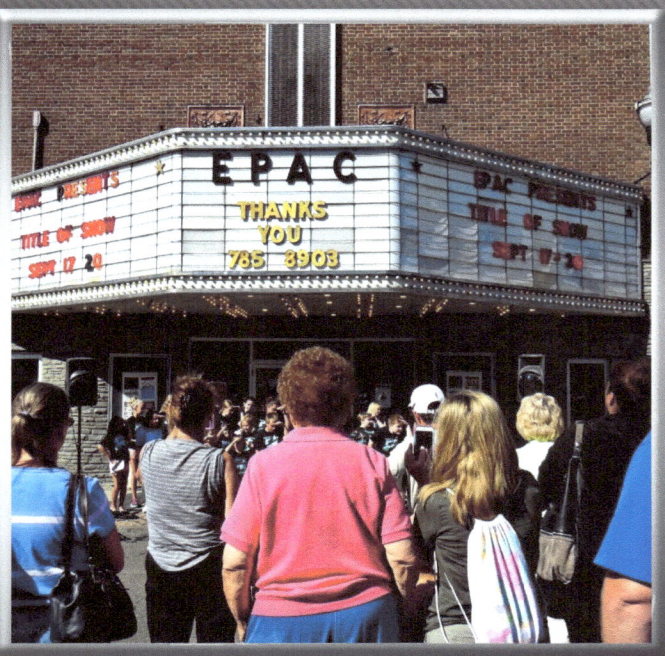
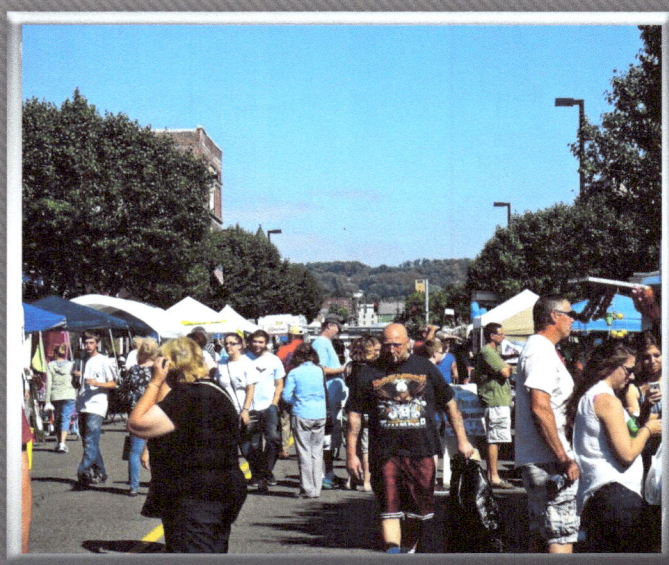

Endicott's Apple Fest

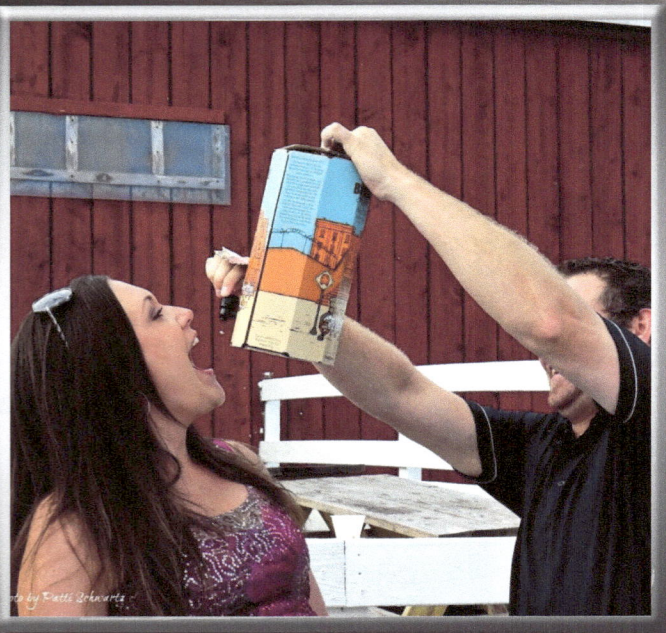
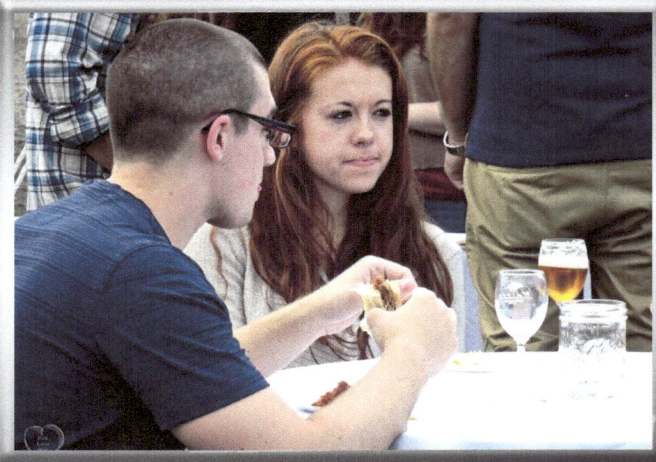
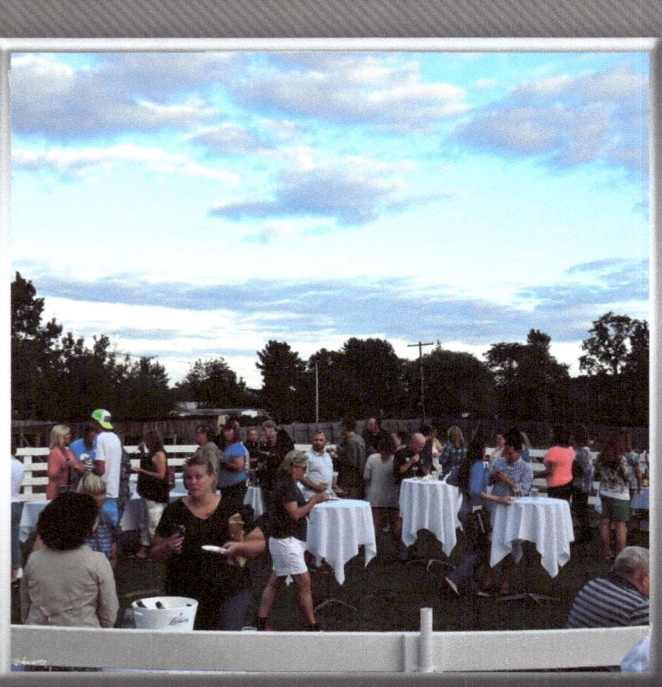
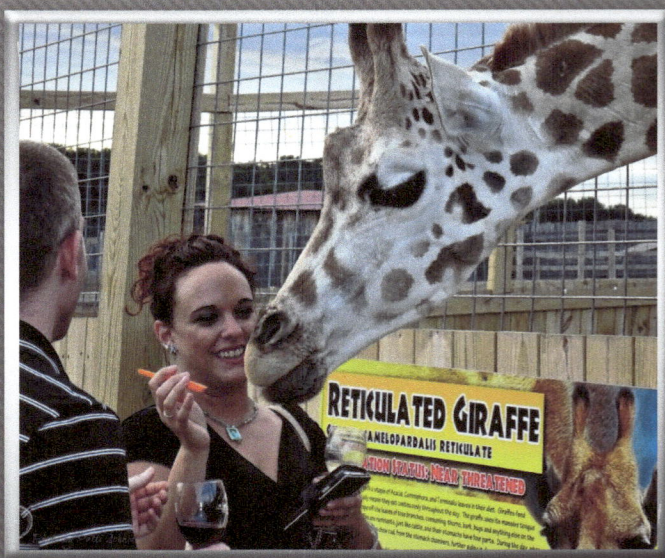

Animal Adventure's Wine for Wolves

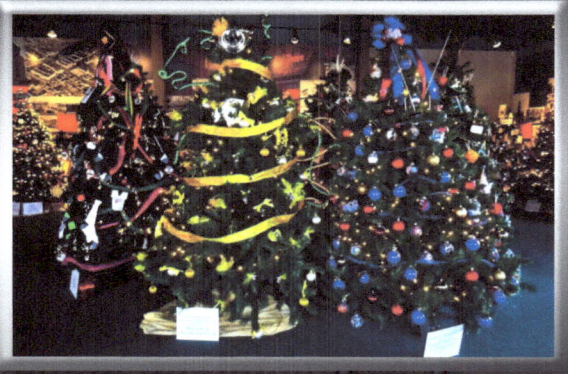
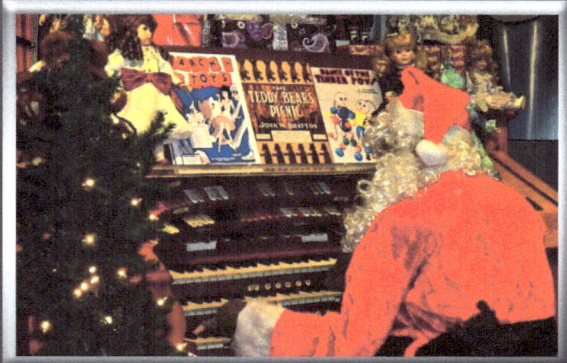
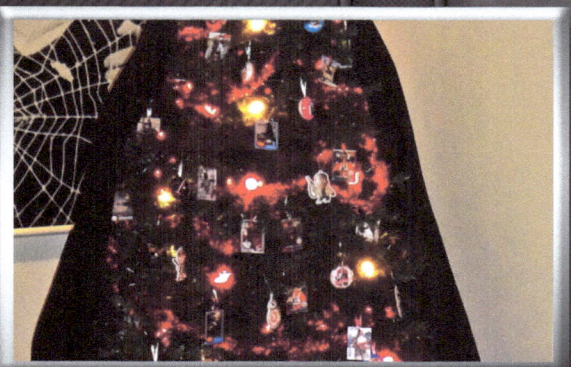
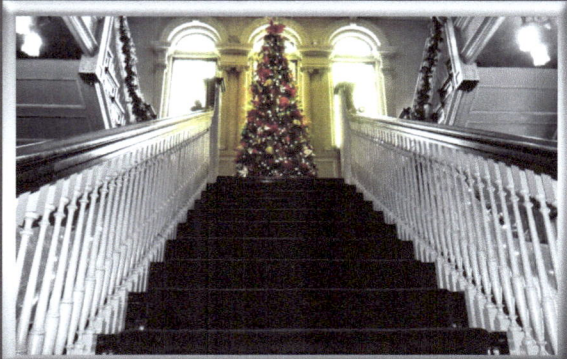
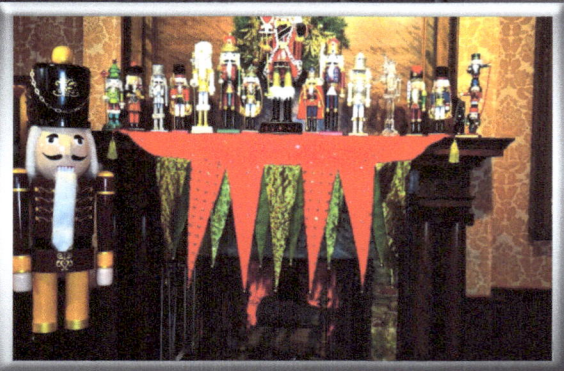
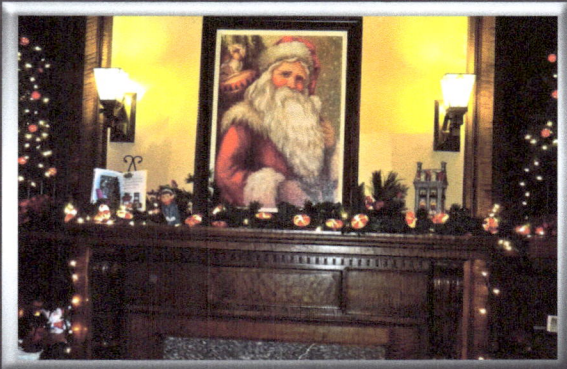

Roberson Museum Home for the Holidays

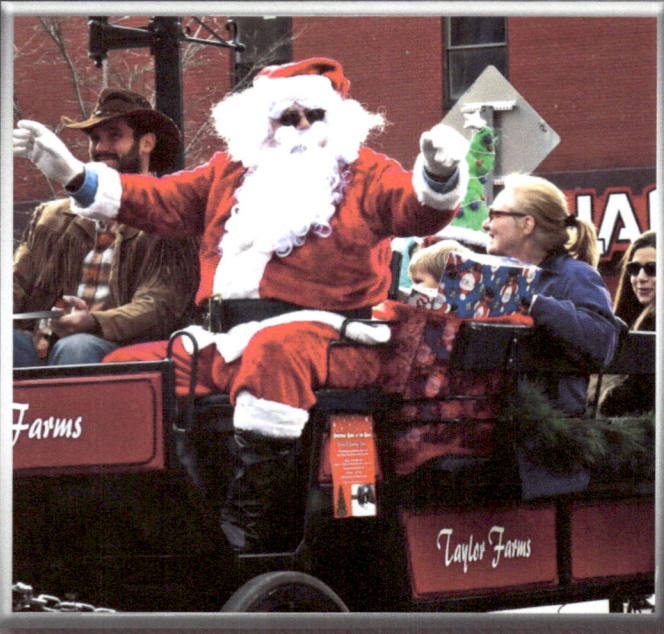
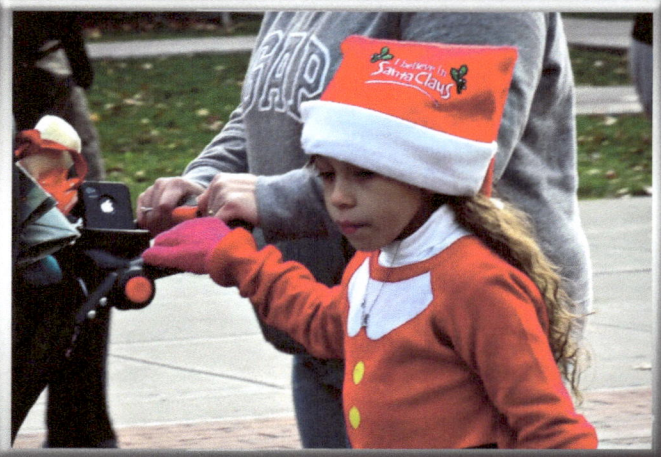
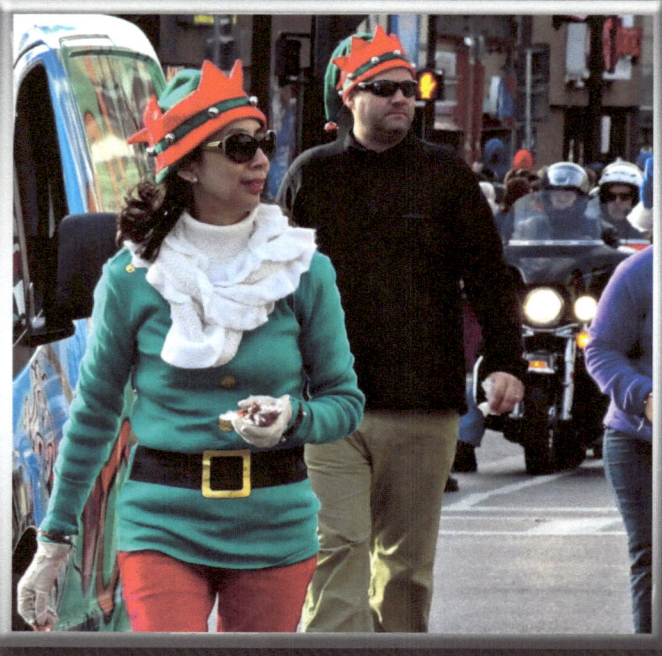
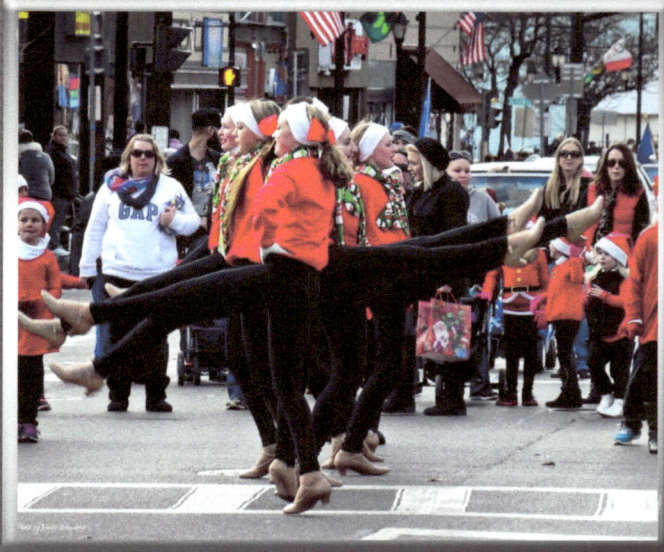

Boscov's Holiday Parade

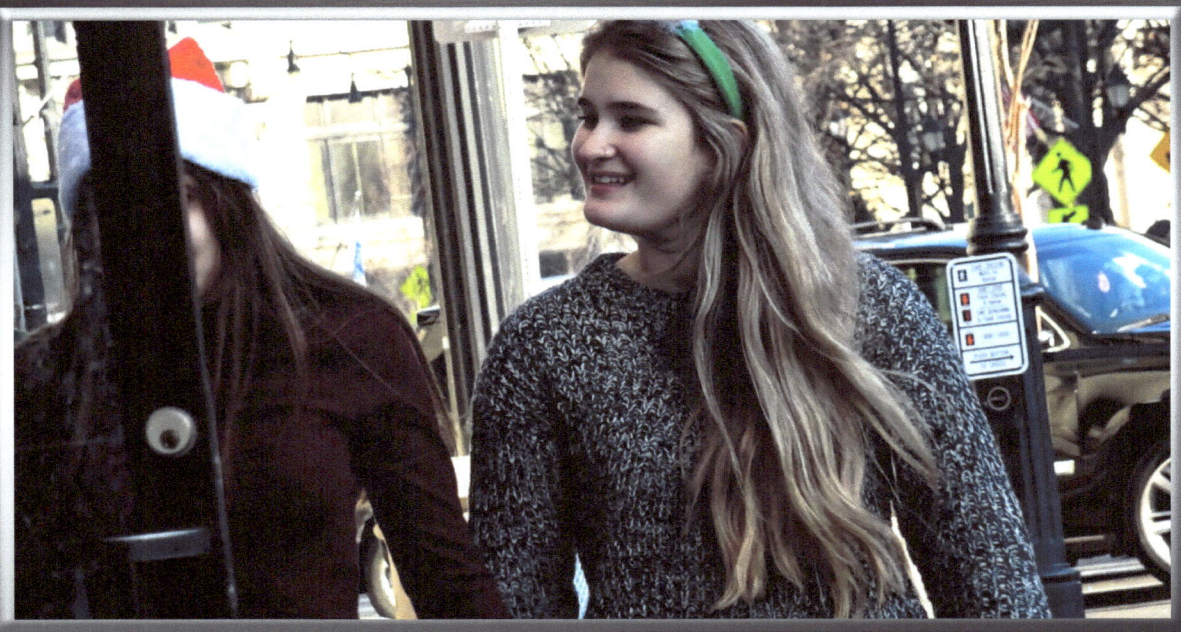
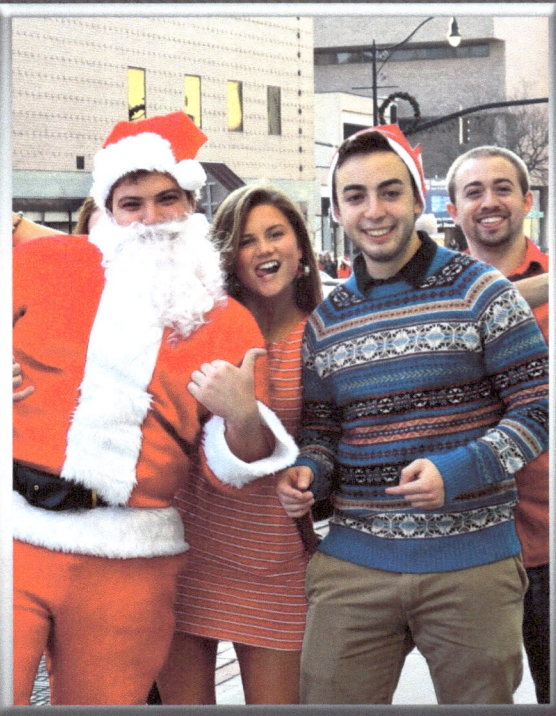
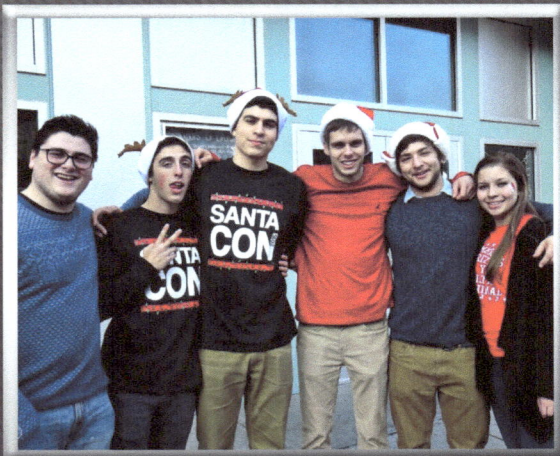

SantaCon

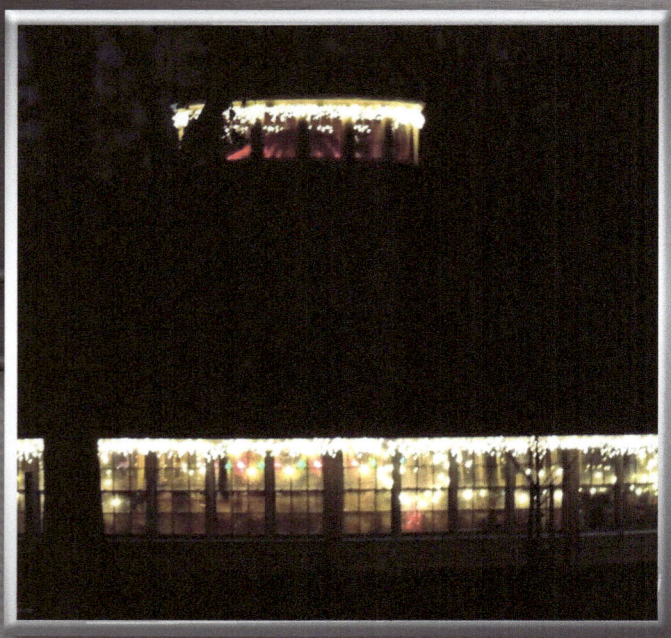
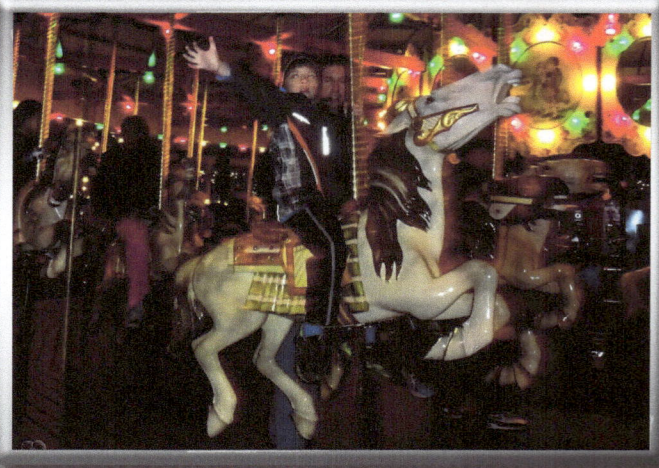
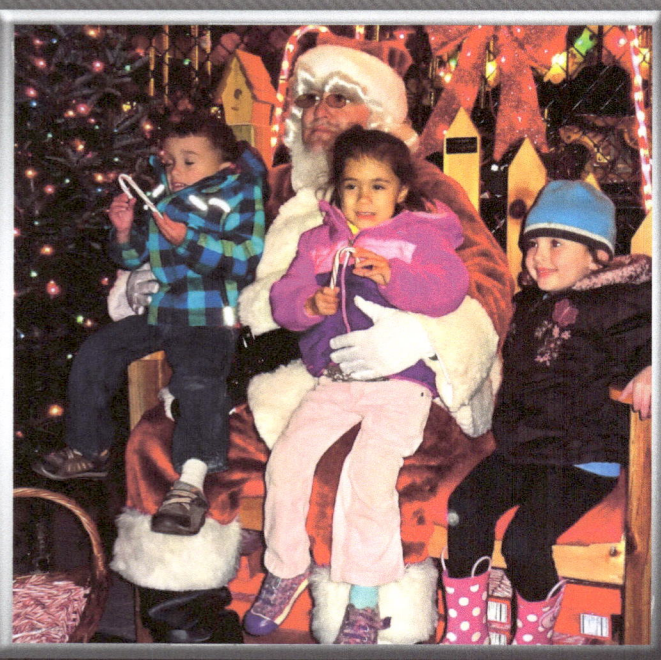
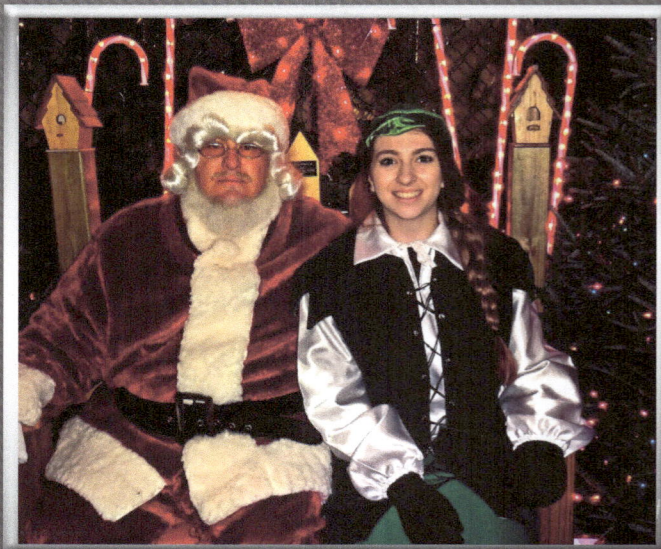

Recreation Park Holiday Carousel Rides

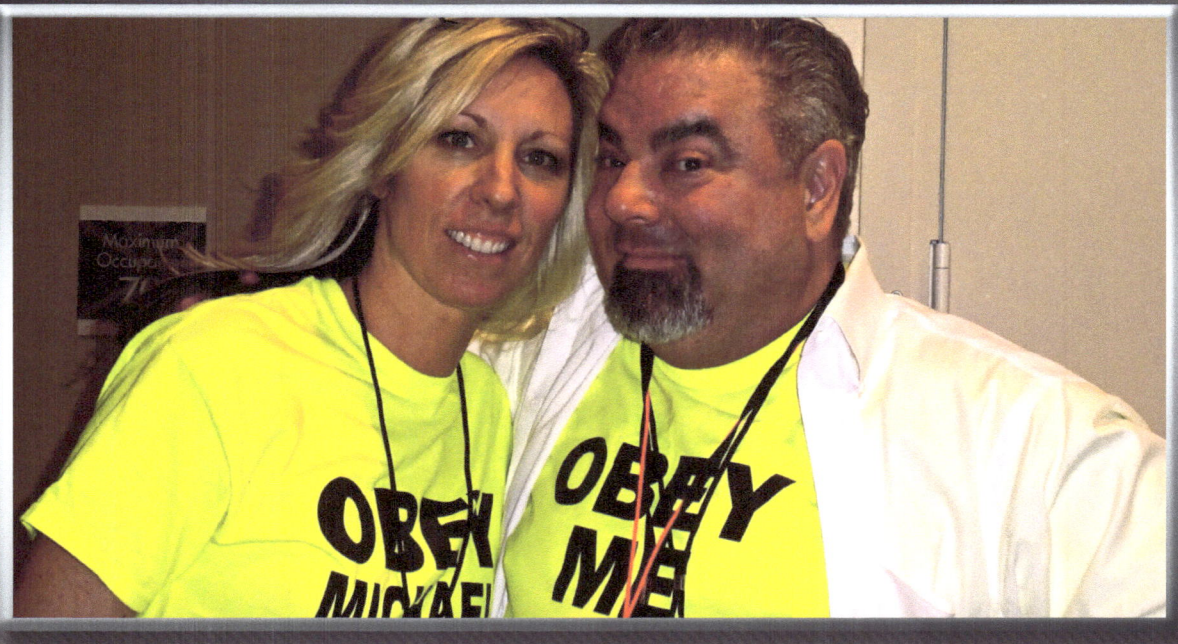
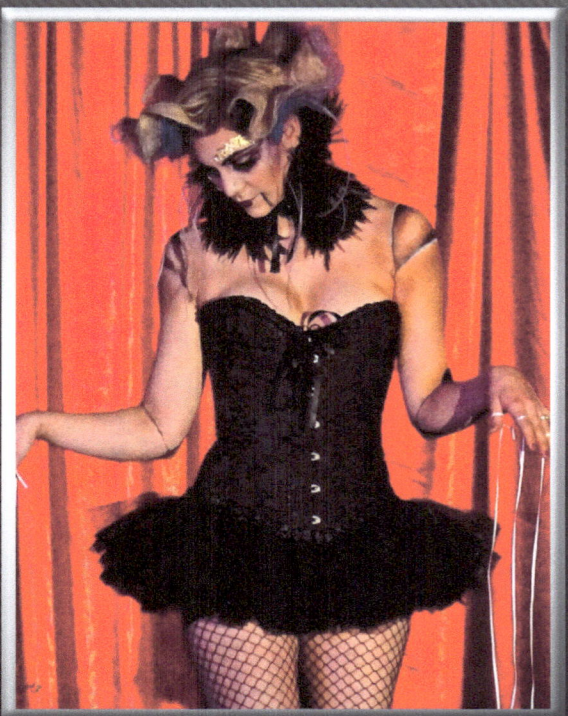
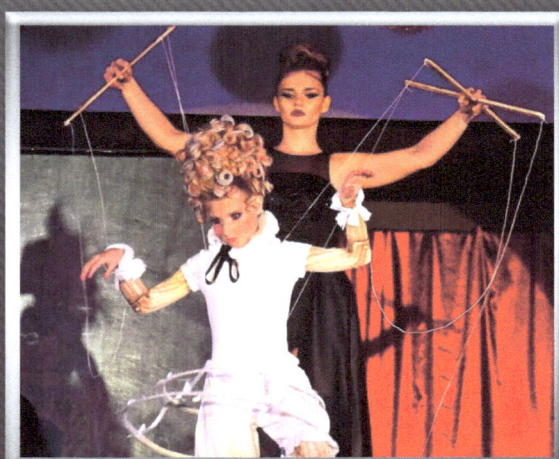

Hair Warz

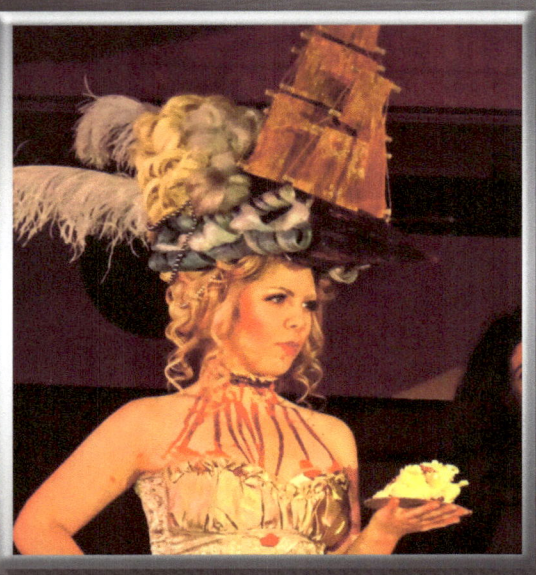
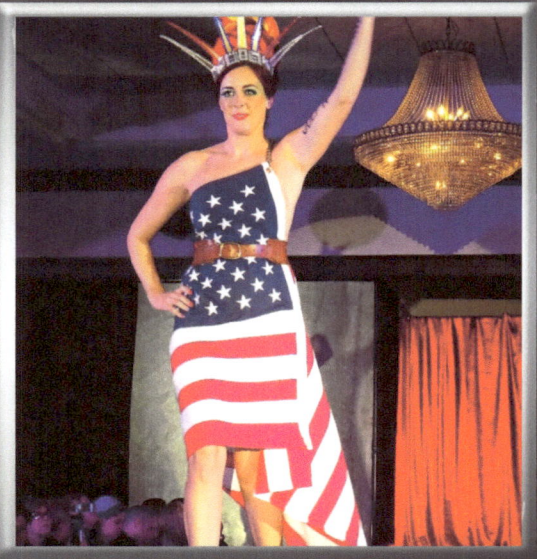
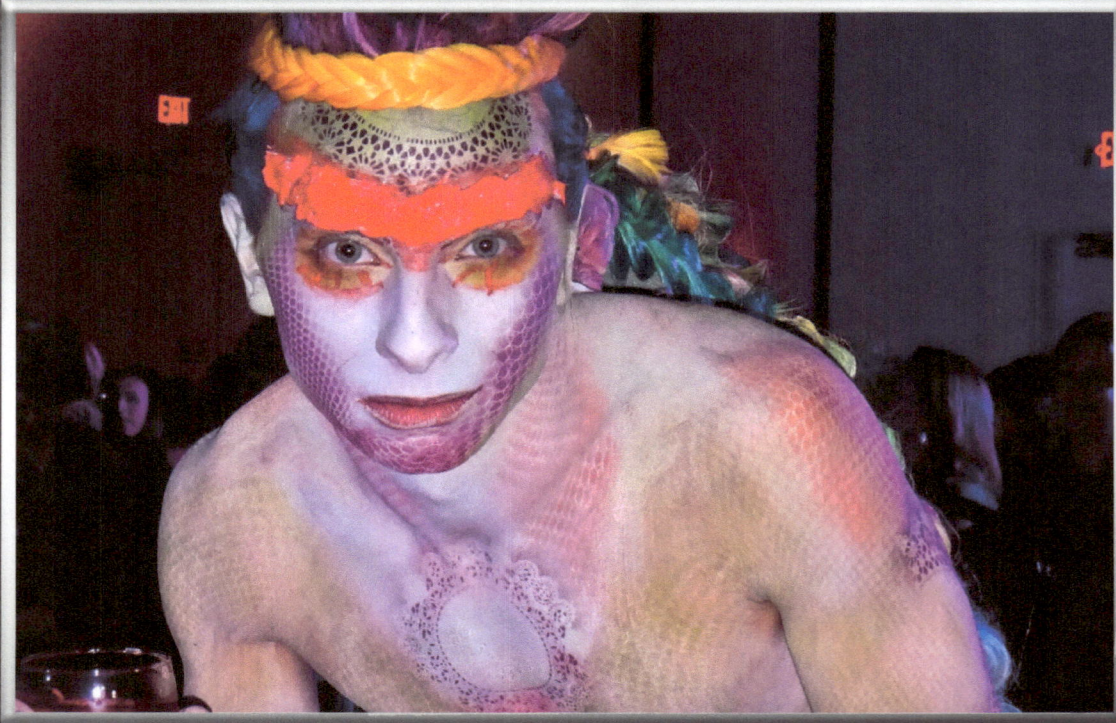

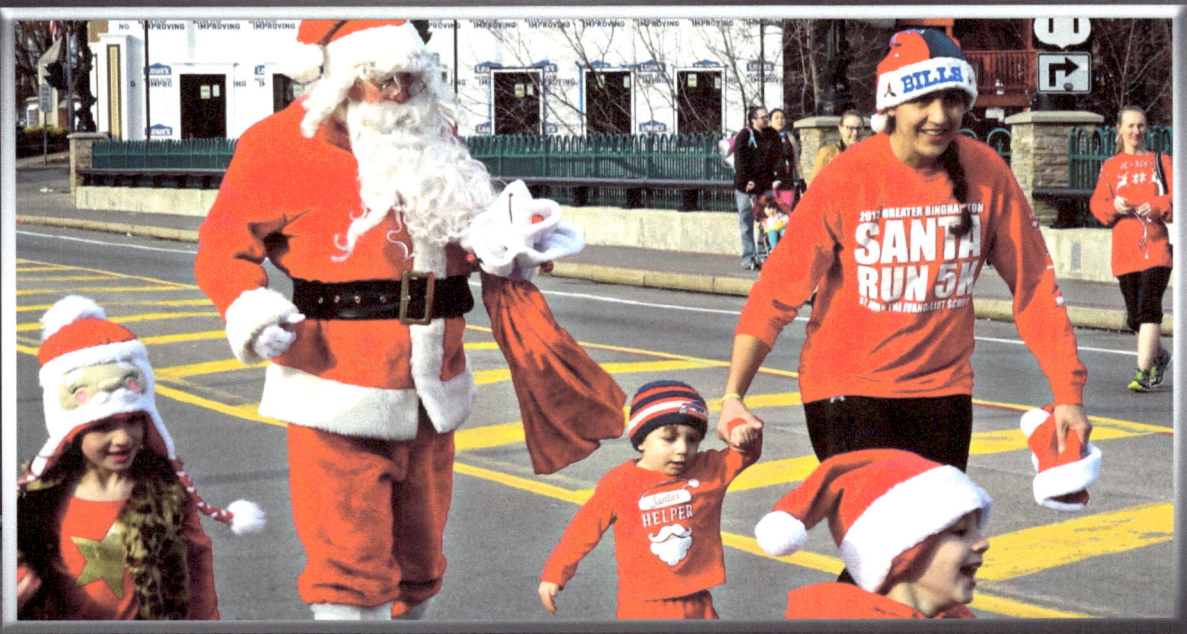
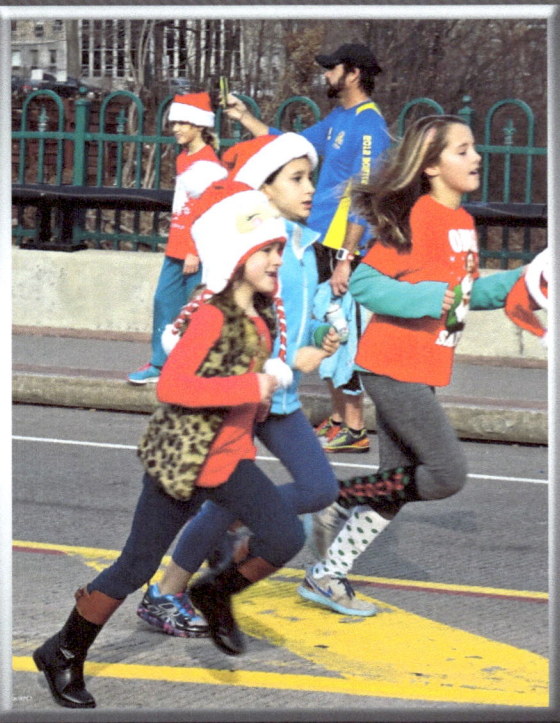
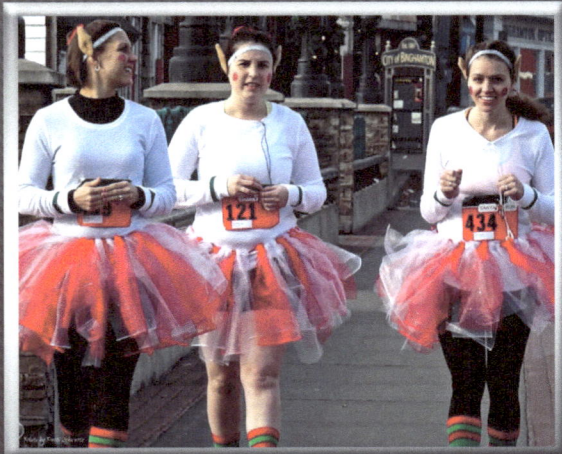

Santa Run

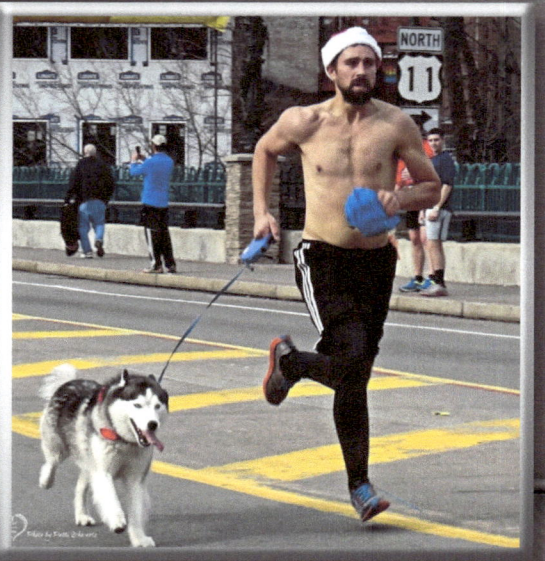
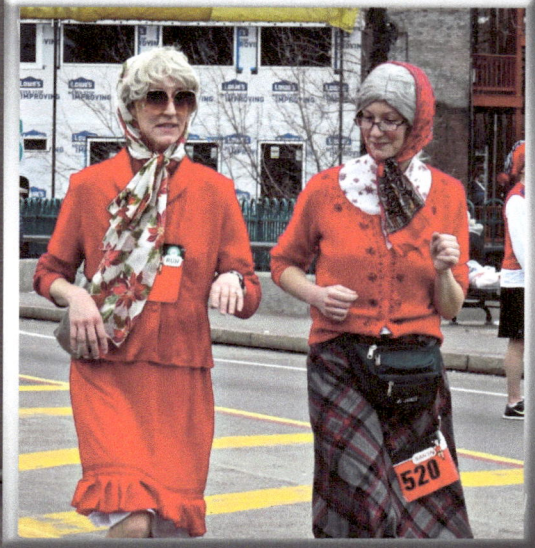
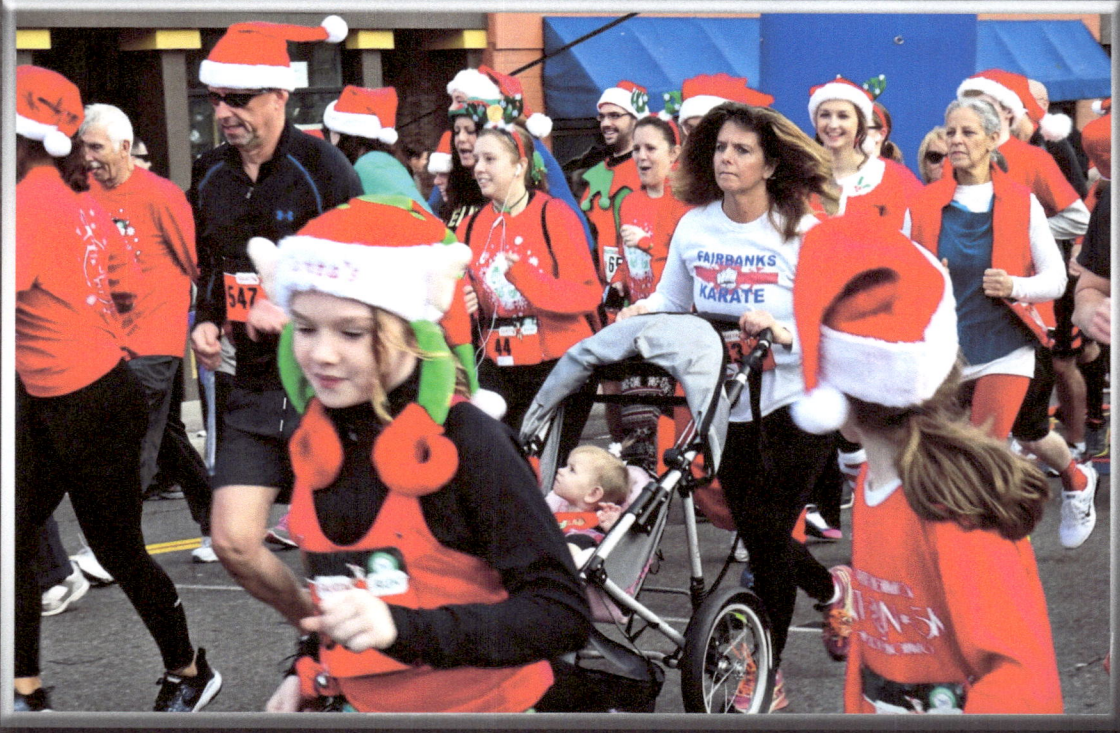

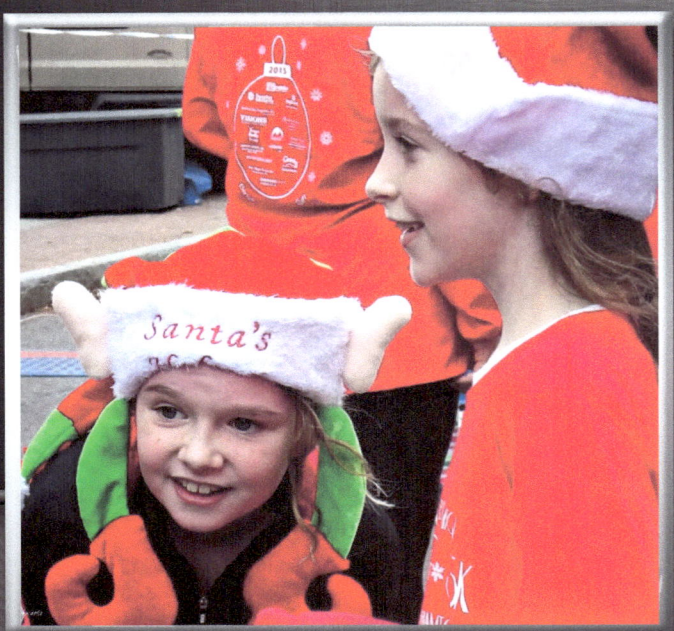
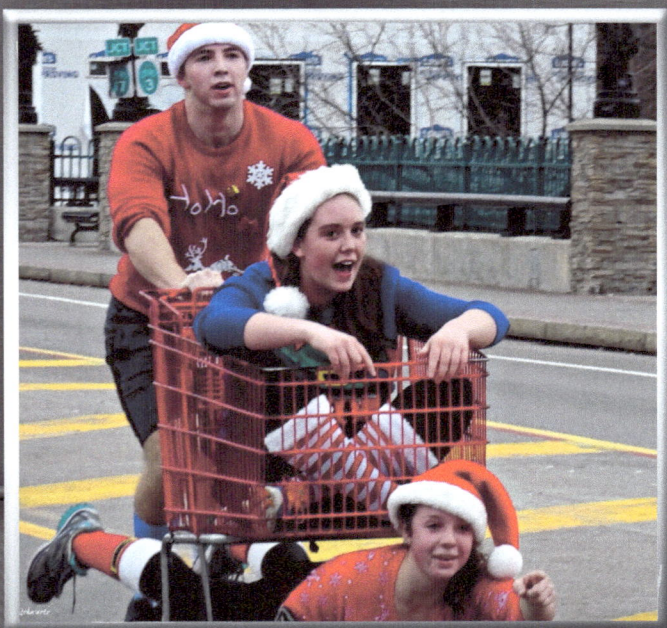
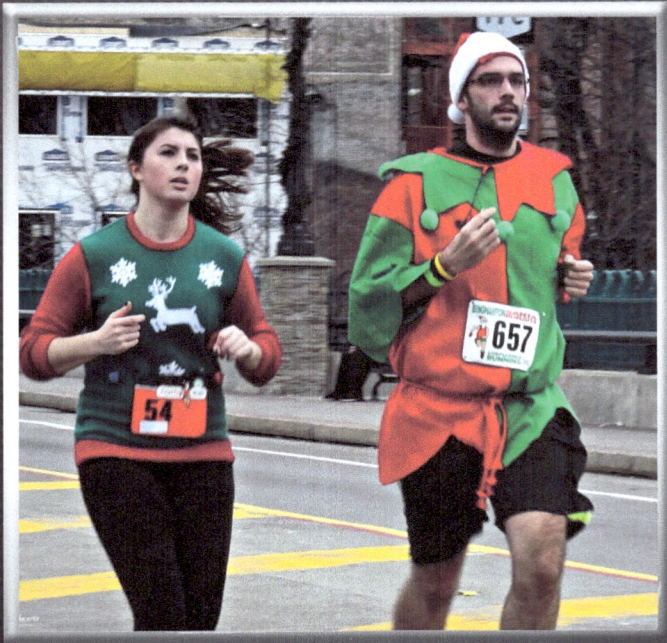
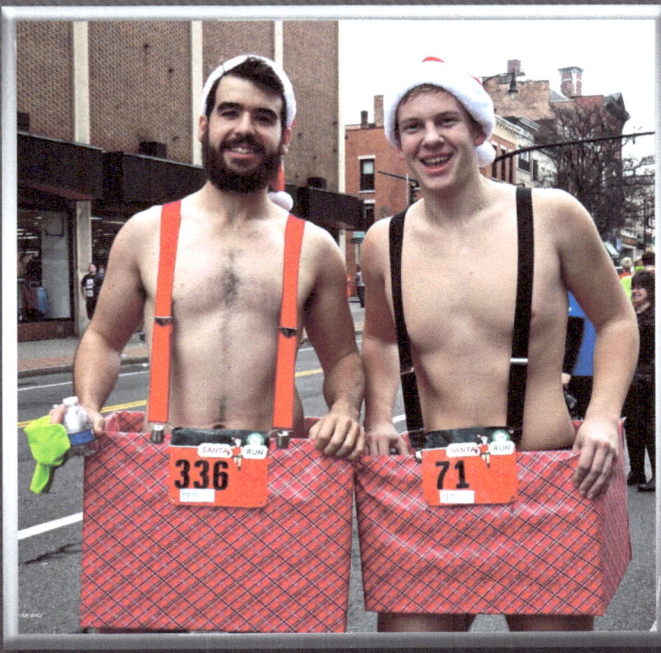

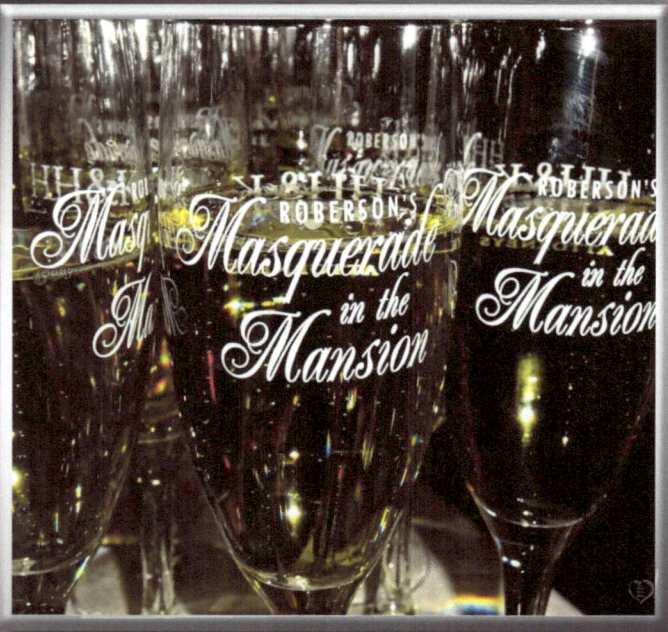
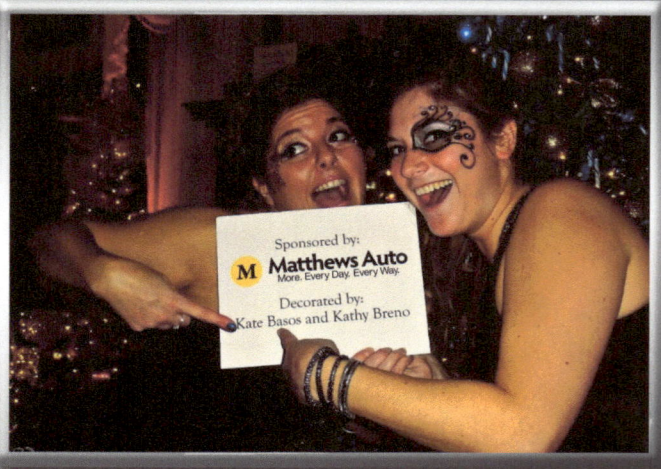
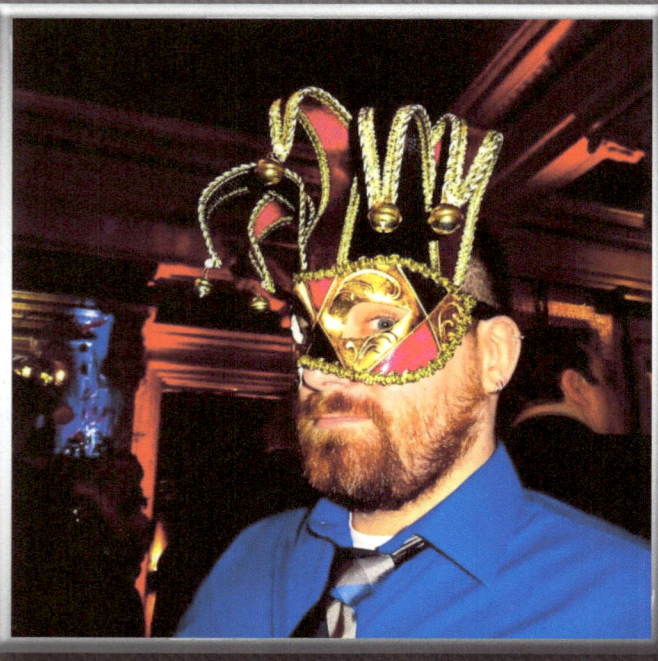
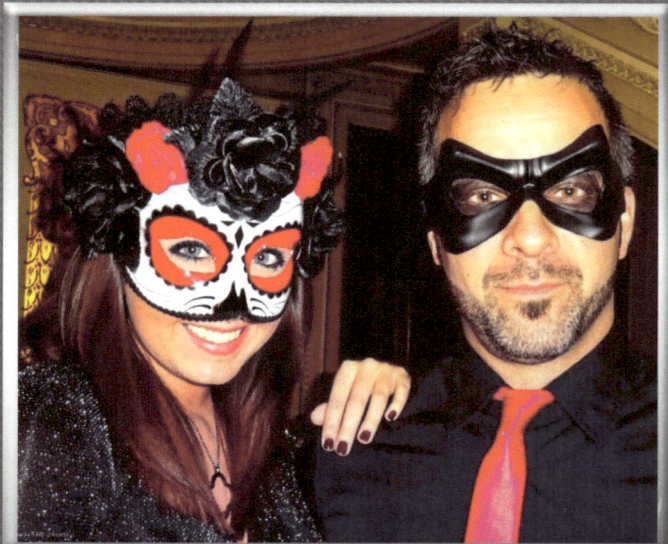

Roberson's Masquerade
in the Mansion

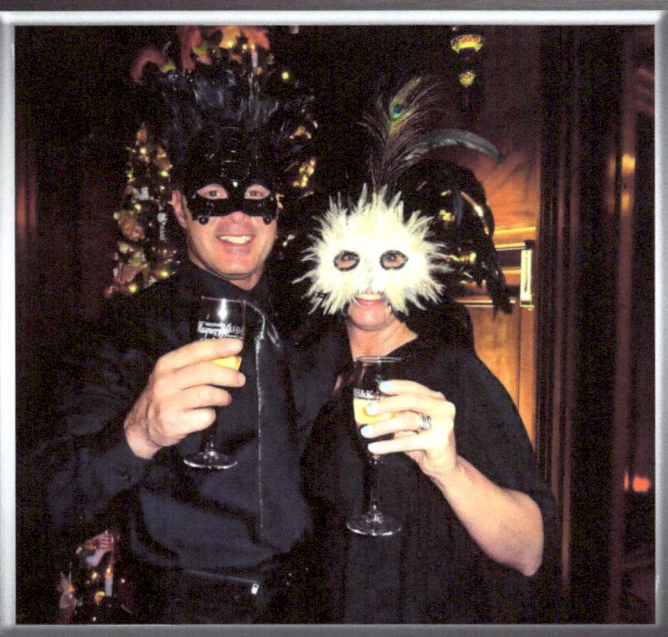
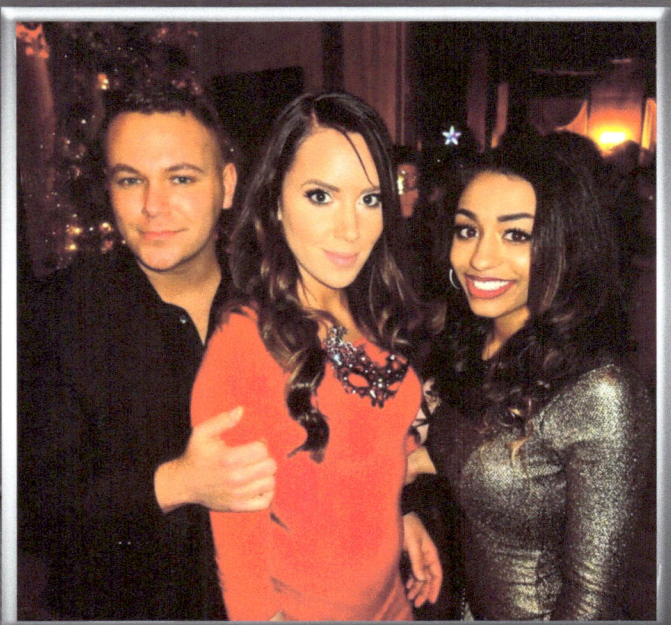

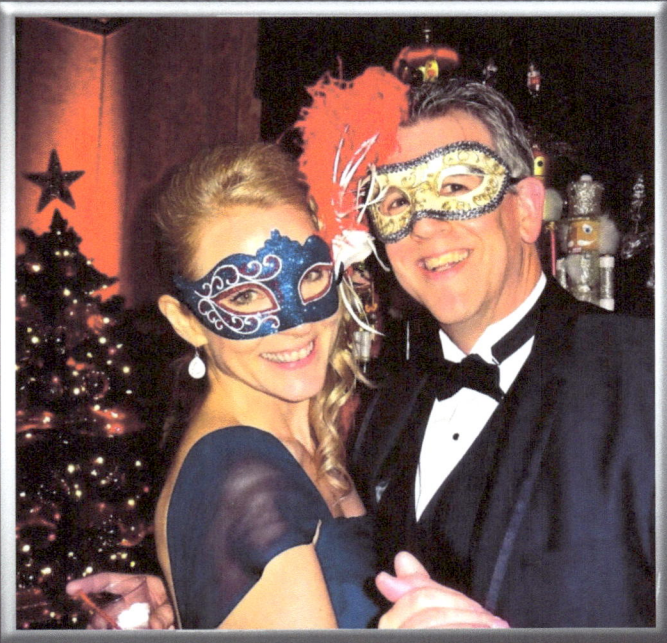

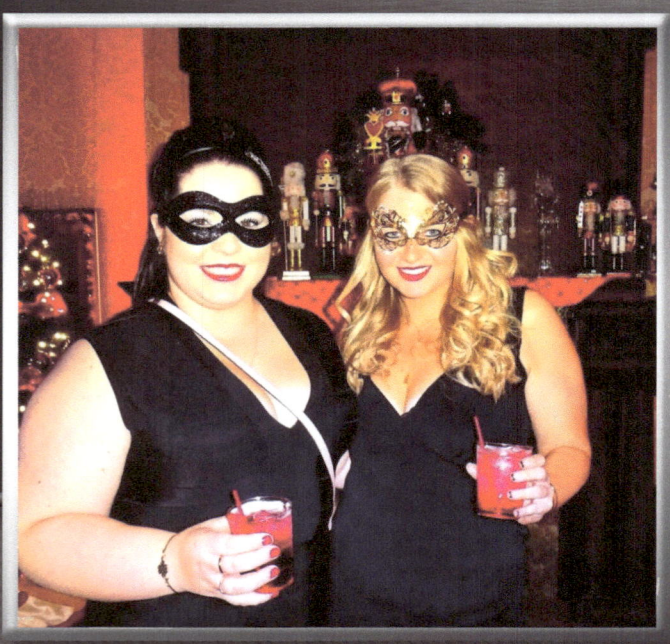
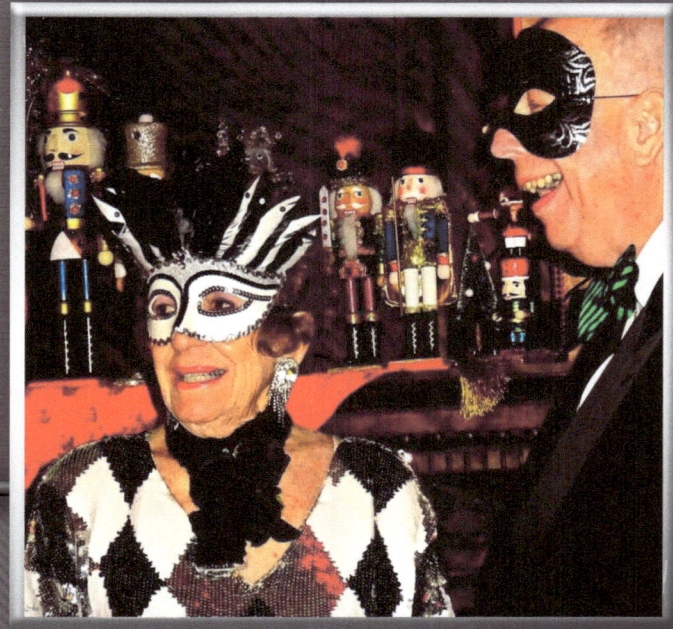
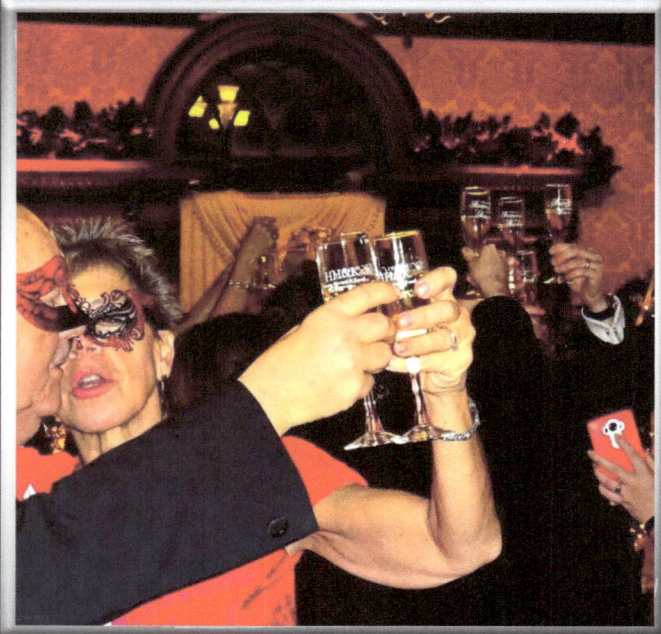
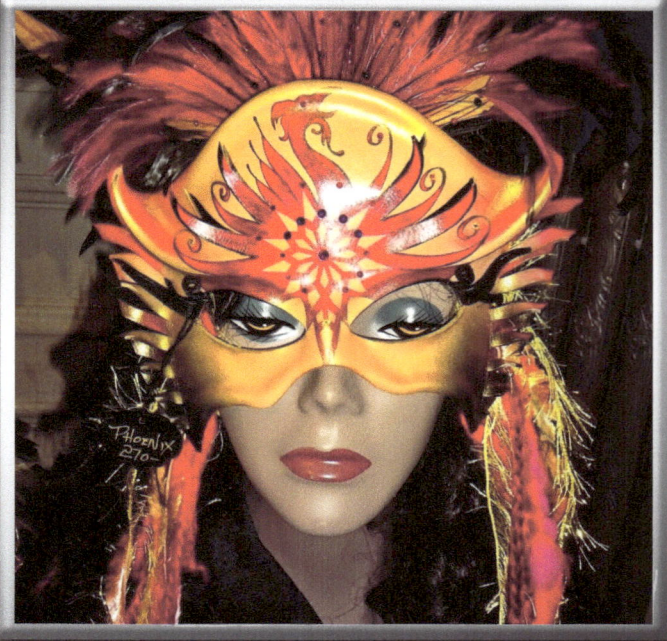

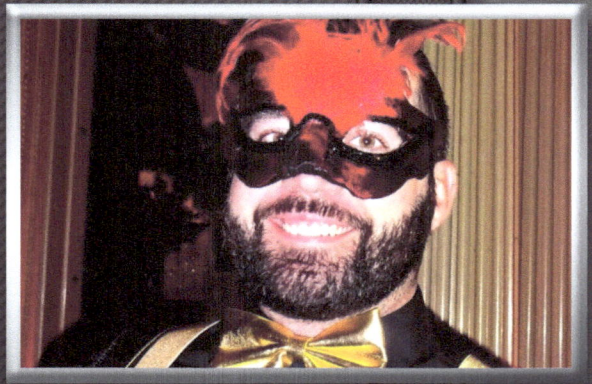
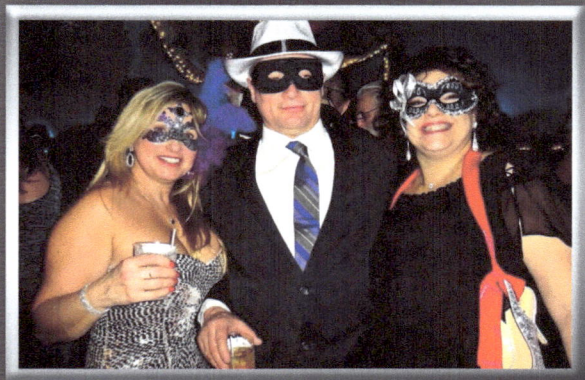
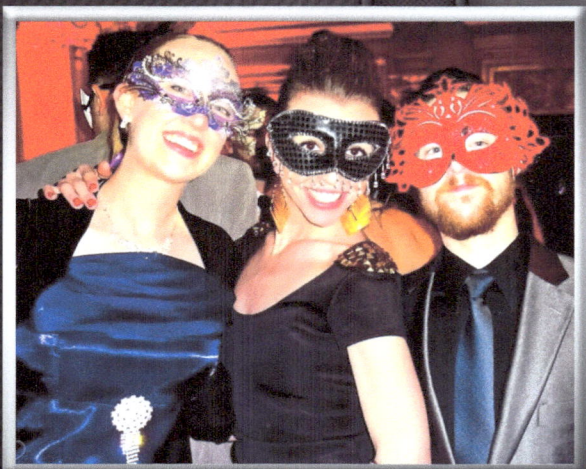
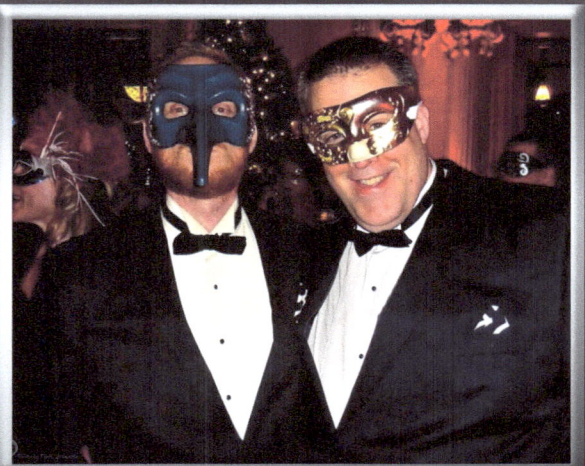

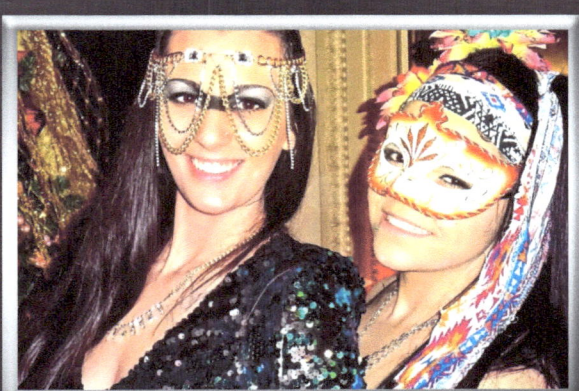

www.ingramcontent.com/pod-product-compliance
Lightning Source LLC
Chambersburg PA
CBHW051211220526
45473CB00003B/989